The Diary of a Lockdown Mum

Written by Paula Love Clark

Illustrated by Gemma Pepper

The Diary of a Lockdown Mum

DEDICATION

For Harriet, Lauren and Zac – a book per brick. I will not break my promise x

To Anne,

Thank you for being such a lovely and supportive friend; always encouraging and always having my back.

I am so grateful to you 💛.

So hope you enjoy this book and giggle in all the right places 😊.

Love ya!

Paula 🐝

Table of Contents

Foreword

Paula Love Clark is the author of two poetry books and one self-help book. On a call with Paula one afternoon in January 2021, we chatted about her plans to write a second self-help book. During the conversation, I asked her how she was coping with lockdown, being a single parent with three kids, (two at home) home schooling, being a 24/7 chef and with the new addition to the family, a puppy. So, three hours later, just kidding, I advised Paula to put the self-help book on hold and write about her experiences as she'd described them to me. Paula did just that, and two months later her new baby - The Diary of a Lockdown Mum – has arrived.

David P Perlmutter

Check out David's books on Amazon

https://www.amazon.co.uk/David-P-Perlmutter/e/B0089Y9DW0

Follow David on his blog **http://davidpperlmutter.blogspot.com/**

Follow David on twitter **https://twitter.com/davepperlmutter**

The Diary of a Lockdown Mum: Introduction

Meet Penelope Wood, a 47 year-old single mum of three kids, fur mummy of one puppy Labrador, and pretending not to be an aquatic mummy of two very neglected tropical fish.

Before the dreaded virus came and rocked the world of 2020, Penelope wore two career hats: one working with a production company and the other as an establishing costume designer. Both freelance and both resigned to fall within the cracks of government assistance when her work disappeared into the pandemic ether.

But Penny being made of tough stuff, dug deep within her Welsh knickers and found a pen and notepad and started to write, thus pursuing a childhood dream borne many moons ago on the hills of a little village in the depths of the Welsh Valleys.

The first lockdown came and felt more like a holiday. The second came and bit at her growing cankles, but distractions kept her sanity in check. Then the third lockdown, with the closing of schools, was almost the undoing of Penny Wood. Could she manage this new homeschooling hell? Would Ms Wood sail through these choppy waters of fractions, emptying of cupboards from bored hands and mouths (including her own) and the constant, deafening chatter of Xbox humdrum? Would she emerge as victorious Queen or jailbait mum?

Bring on the gin and let's take a look inside her Diary to find out. Hic!

Day 3895 of lockdown... or thereabouts.

Dear Diary,

We have no food. The dog ate the carpet out of desperation. The kids ate the fluff out of each other's toes. I lick the toes afterwards, for scraps and flavour. I know, it's a mum thing - we always put ourselves last! The dog licks everything just in case anyone has left a slither of anything behind. And then he barks.

The bills and statements have piled up. Good job because I sold the furniture three months ago and the stack of bills, letters and old magazines are making a great substitute chair. If only I realised how useful getting that Tatler subscription would end up being. Twelve issues for ten pounds – seemed such a bargain at the time and to think I only bought them for the free face cream and yet here they are now, forming part of the house interior! They're not very comfy, but it's a solid publication and a little comfier than the bare floorboards. Did I mention that the dog ate the carpet?

I managed to secure a weekly 'arrangement' with a guy who works in the wine department of a busy supermarket. Gal's gotta do what a gal's gotta do. The fumes from my breath fuel the car for those momentous trips to the food bank. I don't worry about stinking of cheap, alcoholic beverage, since it's the eau de cologne of the food bank queues these days. Long, long queues and there's always a dog barking. What is it with those dogs?

Winter is upon us. We have heating until next month. I made the decision between paying the heating and feeding the kids. A few months of toe fluff licking would be good for them. Besides, during the first eight years of lockdown, they lived on ten meals a day and a never ending supply of crisps, chocolate, biscuits, cakes and all things fat and sugar. That takes me back. Ah...the first year of lockdown: golden memory moments. Those were the days... Will someone shut that damn dog up?

'Mum? Mum? Get up!'

'Whaa...?' I awoke with a start. My eyes shot open and the familiarity of my bedroom came into view. Had I been dreaming? It seemed so damn real. Did I really dream that I was writing in my diary? Am I writing in my sleep now? No surprise, since the only opportunity to write is after 10 p.m., when the kids are finally in bed. Besides, I did fall asleep writing: flipping pen has ink blotched over my favourite white duvet.

No clue what the time was, I retrieve the phone hidden under my pillow and squint at the face for the clock. I definitely need glasses. Or at least to wear the ones I already have. The numbers glaze into view – 7.43 a.m. No wonder the dog was barking. I am usually up by 7 a.m!

'The dog's been barking for ages Mum. Didn't you hear him? He's soooo loud!' Lily shouted from her room. I was still one foot in and one foot out of that weird dream. Urgh. I shivered as I threw off the memory. 'I hope it never gets to that!'

'What?' Lily peered round the corner of my door. My 15-year-old's face dropped in incredulity that I dared to try hold a conversation with her at this dreadful, god-forsaken hour of the day.

'What?' I grunted back, whilst looking up perplexed from my warm, inviting and not ever wanting me to leave, bed.
'You said something...'

'Did I?' *did I say that aloud?* I shrugged. And yawned loudly. Lily rolled her eyes and walked out.

'You *are* getting up to sort the dog out aren't you Mum?' she said before vibrating the house with the slamming of her bedroom door.

'Oh can't you? I'm just so tired this morning.' I moaned to no one but myself. I genuinely felt more exhausted waking up this morning than going to bed the night before.

'No. I'm tired. I didn't go to bed until late. I was watching a horror film and it genuinely creeped me out.' came the muffled and moaning voice from behind her door.

I sighed. Teenagers! I glanced at my phone again. I ignored the messages from various apps and social media. Nothing to excite, so I slumped back onto my pillow and stared up at the ceiling: Groundhog Day once again. I felt so tired. I hadn't had a lie in for almost ten months since all this began last March. I groaned as I eased my exhausted body out of bed. My back groaned from feeling old and leaning over my bed to write. Plus my left arm ached. Damn frozen shoulder. And damn that dog for barking!

'Don't worry Mum,' said Ben as he emerged sleepily in just his boxers from his bedroom (mental note – same boxers for past three mornings in a row. Must steal and wash). 'I'll let Jimbo out.'

'Oh thanks Ben, you're such a sweetie. I'm a bit slow getting up this morning.' I said with a sigh, oozing myself back under the duvet. Relief flooded over me and I suddenly felt life was going to be just fine again.

'That's okay. I don't mind.' he replied with the cutest, dimple packed grin.

'Ah, you're fab! Thank you.'

'After I let the dog out, can I go on my Xbox? Pleeeeaaase?'

'No it's a school day. Schoolwork first, then tech after 3.30 p.m., if it's all done. You know the rules.'

'Oh but that's not fair! My friend will be on this morning and I told him last night that I would play with him first thing. Come on Mum? Please?'

The dog continues to bark.
'Will someone please go down and see to the dog? I need to sleep!' Lily screamed from her room.

'No Xbox until later. You know the rules – school work first!" I hissed hoarsely at him. 'Now are you going to take the dog out as he's been barking for ages and obviously needs a wee?'

'Nah. I might stay up here and do some reading, you know, for home school. I'll come down in a bit,' he said with a wink and nonchalantly walked into the bathroom, closing the door firmly shut behind him.

'Oi! I need the toilet!' I rebuked as I noticed that the iPad that had been charging outside of his room, was also missing. *That boy and his flipping tech!*

'Gotta be quick Mum!' he shouted back and chuckled. I grunt in exasperation. Deprived of a lie-in and a wee and still the dog barks. I sighed. Already I am looking forward to going to bed at the end of the day.

AT THE VERY BEGINNING:
Saturday March 21st 2020

Dear Diary...

Things are weird in town. Normality is evaporating quicker than a droplet in the Sahara Desert. Like ants on a mission, people scurried under the stench of fear to lock themselves away and hide in their homes. It felt like that little village in the Chitty Chitty Bang Bang film, just before the Child catcher came in to search for the children. Totally surreal.

The supermarkets won the wow factor award, for its rows of empty shelves as people panic bought and crazily stocked up on rice, pasta and – loo paper! Yup, you couldn't make it up! I mean, what is it with the lack of toilet paper? Sourcing the stuff is like searching for King Solomon's legendary mines!

It's all so confusing. Nobody knows anything except there's this nasty virus out there and the news is all drama, doom and gloom. I despise feeling so negative and in shock, but I find myself drawn to the headlines and glued to each passing comment, or piece of journalistic reporting on anything remotely connected to the subject.

I'm absolutely gutted about the loss of my work projects. Really and truly bummed out. I sobbed earlier after the kids left to go to their dad's. I'd been trying to be so brave and tough and not show them how scared or worried I am. If I don't work, how can we survive? And there's no kidding myself that the projects would return anytime soon. They've either completely disappeared into the ether, or cancelled. Some are on hold, but for who knows how long? It takes ages to network into those production teams and shows and now...?

The situation in shops is the craziest though. I'm amazed by how some people are panicking and how self-thinking many have become. I saw a mum struggling with two young kids, stare incredulous at the empty pasta and rice shelves, and an old man with a look of absolute horror at the empty shelves that once held rows and rows of toilet paper. Still not getting the loo paper thing!

It's just so surreal. Everything that was once accepted, feels naughty, wrong or simply forbidden. Going to coffee shops, out to restaurants or pubs, meeting up with friends, visiting family, travelling, even giving hugs. Blimey, anything really that doesn't involve staying in our homes by ourselves or with our immediate family, have all been restricted or cancelled. I kind of understand, but at the same time, it just feels unreal and inhumane almost. Not to hug or touch each other in order to save lives? Mind-boggling.

How do I feel about all of this? Not sure. I have no work now and have no other places or distractions to go to. Gosh! How strange to say that, when I was having the busiest few months to date, of my entire working life. It's all a load of poo really. ☹

But there's nothing I can do about it. No point falling apart and crying myself to sleep at night. Most people in my professional and social network are in the same boat as me.

So I've decided I am going to just chill this weekend before the kids are back. Watch some Netflix, lounge in my PJs, eat too much crap, have long baths and go for a walk – all the things I rarely get time to do on a normal weekend. Who knows when I will next get a lie-in, or some headspace? Diary, this is going to be a strange time for sure and I think you are going to become an escape place for me in all of this.

Sunday 22nd March

<u>4.30 p.m.</u>

Well Diary, I almost had a full day's peace. Saskia was kicked out of her digs after a big argument with her horrid landlady. Early hours this morning, there she was, taxi at the door and sobbing her heart out - a pale and spotty 18 year old sobbing on my doorstep. Glad the other kids aren't here. It's funny how things work out isn't it? It was only last week I was complaining to her godmother that I hadn't seen her for ages. That'll teach me!

She came feeling rotten poorly and with a smoking addiction. Nice times ahead for me then. The resistance to my parenting that drove her to London and independent living eight months ago, also arrived back at my door, but with added attitude and some. Whilst pleased that she finally came home, I was not so pleased with the accompanying teenage lip.

She cried intermittently whilst spitting in rage at the inconvenience of the circumstances that led her back home to me. I offered her my bedroom until we sorted out new accommodation (the joys of living in a sardine spaced house), but she wanted to sleep the first night on the sofa. She couldn't switch her brain off she said, so she stayed up watching films and crying on the phone to her boyfriend.

At least I finally got a lie in!!

Monday 24th March

<u>11.15 a.m.</u>

Kids not coming back until tomorrow and there's talk of an impending national lockdown. What does that mean, everything and everyone locked down? It's never happened before. I don't usually watch the news, or indeed, the television at all, since adverts annoy me and I rarely find anything to watch that grabs my attention. However, for the past few days, I've felt like a flipping media leech, clinging onto anything with the words, 'virus' and 'lockdown'.

Social media is going into overdrive. So much talk of stocking up and especially of buying loo paper, pasta and alcohol. Pretty much the essentials for a few weeks locked up at home it seems. *Wait? Did I buy any alcohol?* Damn I forgot! I'm not a big drinker at home. A bottle of white can last a week and a bottle of red up to a month. I get so bored of drinking by myself. Hence I do the drinking when out in London, which roughly equates to three to five times a month. Though when I was dating that publishing director last year, it was more like three times a week. It was bliss! Groucho Club this, Soho House that. Oh how I miss the glamorous

London life and of course being treated so well on those dates. I don't miss him though.

So Diary, I took a look at my alcohol shelf earlier. Blimey, talk about alcohol poverty! One half bottle of port from two Christmases ago (on offer as I remember), an eight year, old almost untouched bottle of Martini (I mean, who likes Martini?) and a third of a bottle of merlot that was at least a month old. I was saving it for making spaghetti Bolognese, but everyone's off mince these days.

6.45 p.m.

Saskia finally woke up around 2 p.m., so I took her shopping. Flipping heck, £98 later! I should have gone whilst she slept. Considering she lived in digs and has no income, that kid has expensive tastes. At least I finally bought a couple of bottles of on-offer wine and a half bottle of gin. Not sure why I bought the gin. I have a real hang up with it after a nasty break up with my ex, but this was on offer. And it's pink! Can't turn down a pretty looking bottle.

Gosh. How shallow is that? Here we are talking about locking the world up because of a pandemic virus and I am buying alcohol purely for the colour of the bottle! At least we have toilet paper and pasta and flour! And now every bloody type of spice that the supermarket sells it seems! One thing the landlady did teach my oldest child, was how to cook sublime tasting African food and apparently that takes a lot of spices that could not be found in *my* food cupboard!

Despite all this weirdness right now, I feel like I am ready to hibernate for at least a couple of weeks. I was pretty exhausted before this anyway. It'll be great to have Saskia around. Haven't seen much of her the past few months. I'd been nagging her to come see me for ages. Yep…life has a funny old way of working itself out.

9.45 p.m.

Oh yes! Seems Saskia also makes the best cocktails! Happy days!!! I so love a cocktail! Despite the weirdness of the situation, I'm now really looking forward to a little break from the norm! Gin cocktails definitely help. Perhaps I should call them 'gin o'cocktails'? Now that'll really spice the coming days up!

Wednesday 25th March

11.40 p.m.

Can I wake up yet? Is this all for real? We just entered an unknown period of national lockdown. No shops, no travel, no socialising and no old life. And my kids aren't coming home yet either. Their dad has decided to keep them for the next three weeks since he feels it's a risk to bring them back in case Saskia has the dreaded virus. She hasn't been feeling well. I'm bereft. I've never been more than 2 weeks without them. How can I cope with three and a half weeks?

And I get severe chest infections. What if S does have it and I get it and am really poorly? Who is going to look after me? What if I end up in hospital? Panic setting in now. Rum! Of course, I should get some rum for my chest. Or brandy. Supermarkets are open so I can always go get a bottle, just in case. But what if I already have the virus? I can't go and possibly infect everyone just to buy some brandy! Argh. What a dilemma. I need it to help kill the chest cough I haven't yet got, but might get! Wait a minute…James. I'll call James. He works in a wine shop. He can do a drop for me. Phew.

Sorted that emergency. Love rum. And brandy. And wine. I should stock up really. It's going to be a strange few weeks.

Funny how rum makes me so horny though. Weird that Diary. Ah, I have some fun memories with rum. Hehe...

Oops. S just walked in on me to say goodnight and there I sat writing, with a naughty grin splitting ear to ear. Her quizzical face was a picture. She quickly scarpered.

Gosh, thinking about the rum days has definitely awoken a few forgotten about feelings. I might nip downstairs and pour a glass of rum and coke. So what if it's almost midnight? I'm in shock of lockdown and not seeing my kids. I need all the help I can get right now.

Mmm. I wonder where I put BOB? ;-)

Thursday 26th March

Mental note – don't drink rum and coke before going to bed. Was up most of the night with a mind whirring like a car engine. Wiped out today. Just mooched and watched the TV. There's no way I am going to spend my days staring at a box sucking my brain dry.

Feeling very disheartened, with the sense that World War 3 just started. TV is so depressing!

Must get a new hobby and distract my mind. Tomorrow I will brain storm. Today my brain stormed out. Must sleep.

Saturday 28th March

3 p.m.

Not felt like doing much. Reality has hit me and I cannot lie, I've felt pretty down for a couple of days. Went to the doctor yesterday and S hasn't got any of the virus symptoms, but is poorly with tonsillitis and a urinary infection that has knocked her for six. She has antibiotics from my doctor, which should help. She's sleeping a lot. Her skin was so bad when she arrived and despite being poorly, she's already looking better after just a week.

When she's feeling better, I'm going to focus on her and strengthening our relationship. This will be the first time in a very long time for us to spend more than a couple of days together without any other distractions. Really looking forward to it.

I'm also going to focus on myself. I've decided that if I'm unable to work at present, then I will become more creative instead. What else can I do? What are my other talents? I've made a list today of things I'm quite good at and things I would like to do based on the vision board I created in a workshop a few months ago. I only went for the free tea and cake, but it was really useful and I now have a beautiful vision board on my bedroom wall, with all my lifelong goals and dreams pinned up on.

As I looked at my masterpiece board, two words hit out at me – writing and painting. I started painting in January and even sold one to a guy in New York who is moving to Los Angeles this summer. He has lots of connections in the LA film industry and I have a great feeling that this could be serendipity working on my behalf. Plus LA is on my vision board too.

I could write. I have the start of a novel sitting on my Mac from a few years back. In fact, just before the marriage ended, I started attending a writing group. I needed inspiration at the time, as the cracks in my relationship were now so huge that one of us was going to fall in and disappear. Perhaps I could re-visit the story and take a look at what I have written? Who knows how long we'll be in this lockdown for and with most of my distractions now gone, I could really knuckle down and get into it? I could even self-publish? Yes, why not, what have I got to lose?

I'm also going to get fitter and start becoming more mindful, do affirmations and meditation etc. I've wanted to do that for a while and with all the negativity, worry and fear swimming around us right now, it might be a good time to start. Tomorrow I make a plan for my life! Time to take back control and create new dreams despite what's happening out there.

I feel so good about this decision. Yes! It's all going to be wonderful. I am not going to let this crazy situation pull me down, but instead, use it to my advantage.

'Saskia?' I call out. 'We are celebrating. Let's make cocktails!'

My girl may not drink very much, especially right now, but she makes the best cocktails going!

'Really? Why Mum? You know I can't drink with the medication and I feel rough.'

'Come on! It's Saturday night and we are going to partyyyy!'

<u>Midnight</u>

That was such a great night. We had such a laugh. S chilled and put on some tunes and I boogied my butt off. She knows I'm a little crazy and loves me getting cocktail tipsy as I just laugh a lot. Despite me being the only one actually drinking or dancing, tonight feels more like being on holiday than being locked up. Yay!

Sunday 29th March

<u>10 a.m.</u>

Hangover from hell. Groan. Partied too hard and at home, with only me drinking. Mustn't let S make cocktails for me again, especially on an empty stomach. Eat first. Lesson learned. Hard lessons learned. Urgh. But I know me – I'll make the same mistakes again and again!

Too tired to write Diary. Can't out of bed. Must do better. I don't think I've felt this rough since I last partied at that conference eighteen months ago: the one where I ended up doing my now infamous party trick. Why am I so embarrassing?

Can't believe I feel like this from drinking at home and on my own! Blimey, how am I going to survive the next few weeks?

Monday 30th March

Started a morning routine. I can't lie in anyway. Damn body clock! Even without a nine year old waking me every morning to tell me his dreams, or at silly o'clock to inform me his duvet has fallen off, I still wake up before 7 a.m. What is it with Ben having to come in and tell me his dreams in the middle of the night anyway? Didn't see that part in the mum contract. *'You shall be at your kid's beck and call, morning, noon, night and anything in between! You shall listen to his dreams, his nightmares, tuck him back in if his duvet falls off no matter what time of night and remind him to wipe his butt, flush the toilet and wash his hands every single time he has a poo!'* I always seem to forget to remind him about that last one. Damn.

I can't complain really, because one day I know I will look back at these times and only remember how cute he was. Right now though, I could throttle him when he wakes me from a very much-needed sleep and always with that one word hollowing out my sleeping brain...'Mummmmm?'

So this is the plan:

20

- Up with the sun. No point setting an alarm as I can't sleep past 7 a.m.
- Write a gratitude list - use the gratitude journal I got two Christmases ago from Helen
- Prayers and meditation to focus my breathing, ground myself and to set me in the right mindful attitude for the day
- Have my detoxifying hot lemon and ginger with honey (must start to like ginger), plus my detox Greens drink. Remember to take supplements, especially Vitamin D, C and zinc right now with this bloody virus
- Exercises for 30 mins and stretches to supple up. Maybe try yoga? I WILL have a toned tummy (or at least have it looking flatter than it does right now. Distended is NOT a good look)
- Write 1-2 hours before midday
- Walk for an hour in the woods. Call friends or listen to a self-help audible book. Get in the right frame of mind.
- Brunch
- Afternoon – write
- Spend time with Saskia
- Try not to drink, eat toffees, chocolate, crisps or anything that will make all that exercising futile!
- Go to bed before 11 p.m.

So Diary, it's 5 p.m…

I was doing fine with this routine until I got to the late afternoon. 5 p.m. is the time I seem to get edgy and bored. This is the time I try to drag S out for a walk. She is still resisting, but if I persevere long enough I know she will relent. It's definitely the time I am hitting the snack cupboard mooching around for something sweet or salty. Dangerous time.

Groundhog Day boredom kicks in around now. And it's only been a week. Strangely, it feels like a holiday, since there is no work, lots of rest and no kids' routines to structure my day. But since there is no beach, I am reminded that this isn't a holiday. Oh, if only there was the hot sun, a beach, a sunbed...

Saskia sleeps a LOT. She sleeps through all sorts of noise. The next-door neighbour's dog barking incessantly, the family that shout not talk at each other round the back, another neighbour round the corner who have decided to get their house re-cladded, the never ending deliveries and supermarket vans and their utterly annoying beep beeping when they have to reverse onto my drive to turn around. She sleeps through it all, until as late as 4pm some days. Perhaps it's because she's poorly, so I won't judge? However, maybe going to bed earlier might help her? It will also benefit me too. She's up until two or three in the morning chatting to goodness knows whom, whilst I try to pretend I can't hear a thing, but with the walls being so paper thin, that's nigh on impossible. Living with teenagers is such fun!

I'm finding alcohol helps with the ear numbing after midnight. I had two bottles of pink gin gifted after I told two not-so-secret admirers that I had bought myself a very cute half bottle of pink gin. I mentioned that there was very little alcohol in the house, which was true at the time, but after the delivery of the rum, brandy and wine from James, I had enough booze for at least a month. Throw in two hefty bottles of donated gin and some Fever Tree tonic, then I had more drink in the house yesterday, than I had since the time we had 32 bottles of wine left over from our wedding in 1999! Ah, those were those days, when I used to get tipsy on a glass of Babysham.

Mmm. I wonder if I should have mentioned to those admirers that I don't really like gin? Should have said champagne instead. Hah. Since I am hardly the biggest drinker and I currently have a kitchen full of the stuff, this is definitely going to be an interesting few weeks for sure.

Tuesday 30th March

Loving my morning routine. I am feeling so peaceful and calm. From finding forty things to be grateful for, to the Deepak Chopra 21 Day free meditation practise I signed up to and then the exercise routine to keep my body in shape. Things aren't as bad as they could be.

Plus I love my mid morning walk. I walk from the house to the woods and back for my daily hour exercise. I usually call one of four people. This isn't because I don't want to call my other friends as we do message and speak, but these four are particularly helping me on my journey and keeping me from going insane with boredom. I'm trying to figure out who I am right now in this moment of my life and since the old doors have all been forced shut for the time being, I am seeking a new path and I need all the encouragement I can get.

Rosa my spiritual, medium friend is my go to for pouring out my heart and soul about every possible subject matter. She lives nearby but I rarely see her as she keeps herself to herself. I feel she sees the inner me and I can expunge all my deepest fears and joys, existential thoughts and is also someone to whom I can explain my 'what if' seeking questions. Boy do I have a lot of those! She always picks up the phone, even if my energy is low and needy. She is also the one I will sob my heart out to. Thank goodness for Rosa in my life, or I swear would go mad! She's also told me to write. In fact, she has been telling me to write for the past two years.

David my other spiritual friend is in his late sixties, lives in North London and isolating with illnesses that consider him vulnerable to catching this virus. He seems to see where I am going and his words of wisdom are 'stay on the bloody train and stop trying to get off at every flipping platform'. He kicks my ass back onto the train. He's like my crystal ball and I listen to him. When I am anxious or twisted inside about what the hell is going on, or what the heck my path is, I call David. He has also told me to write.

Jenni, who lives in Yorkshire, is a completely different character. She isn't spiritually wise like Rosa or David and has very little advice for me. In fact, I don't think she has much wisdom at all from what I can tell and if she has, she isn't really using any of it for her own life. She simply is someone I can bounce life's shit off, as well as talk about my goals and the writing. We met many years ago at University and have stayed in touch off and on throughout the years. I can honestly say that she has a wild life, lives right on the teetering edge and definitely has more issues than me and that's saying a lot! Hence we usually have great conversations about all sorts of stuff. And a lot of laughs about sex, guys, toys (!) and all things female!

Finally, the person I call the least often and also the person who makes me laugh the most, is Andy. He's a fairly new contact whom I met at a London Fashion Week networking event last year. He's a 31-year-old music producer living in North London and the biggest tart I have ever met. Once we got past the dick pic he sent me within the first week of messaging, we became solid friends. I think the triple laughing emoji I replied to the unsolicited photo with, was a real ice-breaker. And maybe the comment 'Okay, that's the cocktail stick, now where's the sausage?' might have helped my corner too.

He's hilarious, naughty, extreme and rebellious. Yet he also has the kindest heart and the biggest dreams. And with the loneliness of lockdown and both of us losing a ton load of work, he has become one of my lifelines.

Since I am up at 7 a.m. with the larks, the tits and the bloody cooing pigeons, by the time 6 p.m. finally arrives, I am ready for something exciting in my glass!! Slosh of pink gin, topped with tonic and lots of frozen berries and a dash of mint...well, I could be anywhere in the world. Bliss. Ooh I love a cocktail. I miss my social life so badly!! Going out to fashion events, film festivals, film premiers, exclusive parties etc., was so much fun and I've always loved an excuse to dress up and slap on the make up. However, despite the glamour and glitz, I do see the frivolity and shallowness of that lifestyle. It's not the real world, though I admit that I do miss the girly-ness of the preparations of getting ready. AND of course the cocktails. Did I mention I love cocktails Diary? Hah!

Yes, I miss so many things for sure, but it all seems so irrelevant really when I think of the situation we are in. So cocktail o'clock is a welcome new addition to my day. And since there's currently no school, no kids and no work for me, it can be cocktail o'clock any night of the week! Whoop whoop!!!

Seems I do like gin after all then. Hah!

<u>11.45 p.m.</u>

There is a fine line with drinking at home though. Too much alcohol before bed and you're up for a wee and three glasses of water by 3 a.m.! And thinking you can get back to sleep without doing either, just prolongs the inevitable. Lying there pretending you don't have a parched tongue, spring loaded and curled up like a tensed viper in the burning heat, is futile; it's really all you can think about. Add onto that, a groaning desire to pee, well, that's just bloody hellish. And even when you *do* finally get up to do the necessary and are just about to get back to sleep, the darn morning chorus chirps in and chips away at your peace of mind.

Hellish trying to get some sleep right now anyway, between S and her late night calls, my mind doing overtime with overthinking and the body processing more alcohol and toxic sugar in its system that it has ever encountered before, my sleep patterns are completely out of sync.

There are some bonuses - S is a great cook and she loves nothing more than to cook meals for me: lots of spice and garlic from cooking with her Jamaican and Ghanaian ex-housemates. Cooking is part of her love language and her way of loving on me. She has a nurturing and loving soul. It's so rare to get cooked for and I've been treated now for the past few nights. Delicious! Totally spoiled and not thinking of those extra calories from the added rich foods she sneaked into the basket when I wasn't looking!

Okay, I'm zonked Diary. It's midnight already. So tired must sleep. Miss the kids, but grateful that everyone is healthy and safe.

Wednesday 1st April

Today was crap from morning through to now: a real April Fools' Day.

Argued with S. Told her some home truths about her boyfriend, which was not as well received as I hoped. In my head it sounded maternal, caring and encouraging. I guess it didn't transfer out that way. Lots of screaming (at me) later and many tears shed. I feel awful. It's amazing how kids can make you feel so utterly bereft at times. Feelings of being a failure have flooded me all day. Hate feeling like this ☹

There is nowhere to run, no place to hide. Today I broke the rules and had two walks by myself. I had to go sob somewhere and the space of the woods has become my safe place. Seems my name totally suits my sanctuary place – Wood of the Woods.

I've eaten a whole pack of Jaffa Cakes, half a bag of assorted toffees and half a huge bag of cheesy tortilla crisps (no dip – I was being good). Plus a VERY large gin and tonic and at least 2 glasses of wine. Not a good day at all!

Damn this bloody lockdown. Things could be worse and I know that I am so blessed in my life. For so many people right now, their situations are a hundred times worse, but at this moment, despite knowing that, life feels pretty crap right now ☹

Thursday 2nd April

Diary, I re-set my mind. Can't have dark, feeling sorry for myself days like yesterday if I am going to get through this.

I've started writing my book again! I am pretty sure this is going to go on for at least three more weeks, so I am giving myself no more excuses. I spent the past two days reading what I wrote five years ago. It's actually not bad. I confess that I do have some talent. Though how good it's going to be I don't know. Writing is a tough world and I'm not sure I'm good enough to make writing a living. I told my life coach friend this earlier and he severely berated me for my negative thinking. Apparently I have to tell myself I am an amazing writer, that I can achieve immense success and that I am a Number One bestselling author. Yeah right!

'Adopt some positive affirmations' he messaged 'and say them day and night.'

I tried. I wrote these three down and stuck them on a big A3 sheet of plain paper and blue tacked it up on my bedroom wall next to the vision board:

I AM A BEST SELLING AUTHOR
I AM GOOD ENOUGH
I AM ENOUGH

5 20 p.m.

I was doing okay on saying these until I accidentally deleted a whole chapter of my work and haven't a clue how to retrieve it.

Bugger, shit and fanny flaps! Argh!!!

I was so cross with myself that I stormed round the house like a teenager slamming doors and cursing. I even kicked a box that was lying around in the kitchen, kicking it really hard with my bare foot in anger. I thought it was empty, but it turned out to be full of books and a stereo system that S had retrieved from the garage yesterday. Despite the string of very loud expletives that flung out of my mouth at consistent lightening speed, S still remained asleep.

I think I've lost it. My mind yes, but also a whole flipping chapter: about five and a half thousand words. Argh. And no clue how to get them back. Double argh!

I spent most of the following couple of hours messaging anyone and everyone about how to retrieve deleted work, but to no avail. I'm sure it's possible, but I'm so not techie. In fact, I can't even figure out instructions or even how to work the Xbox! Saskia is better than me at techie things, but having just split from her boyfriend (again) and struggling with her overwhelming feelings of loss, as well as her lack of housing, it's currently like living with a crocodile – constantly watching my step from her snapping mouth.

Tonight we watched a film together. It was her choice and looked a little scary to me, but since she hates my romantic comedy choice films, I decided to give her free rein, on the basis that it couldn't contain senseless murder, torture or mutilation, or I couldn't watch it. Plus I was feeling awful about the way I'd upset her yesterday, so it wasn't only right to be gracious with the remote control and film choice.

Oh my Lord! I was petrified. I mean really, really terrified. I'm definitely getting old, but give me Jennifer Anniston pulling one of her puppy eyed faces to her leading man, over creeps in dark woods with a chainsaw any day. There was definitely torture, mutilation and so much murder.

'Relax mum. It gets better I promise.'

'You said it wouldn't have all that blood with people getting massacred. It's so scary!'

'It's not senseless though...' she laughed with a wink. She is never choosing the films with me ever again!

<u>1.10 a.m.</u>

I was too petrified earlier to even go for a wee upstairs. S went into the garden for one of her forever-long phonecalls. I did want to ask if she would come to the loo with me, but she was already ensconced in a heated convo. In the end, I flicked on all the lights in the house and ran upstairs to the loo, super peed to the point I thought the entire neighbourhood could hear me, then scarpered back down again. I really don't think I breathed during a moment of it!

To take my mind off the blood and gore images I had just witnessed, I put on Disney's *Moana* film again (we watched it two nights ago). Then to continue the distraction effort, ate copious amounts of crisps and most of a box of Jaffa Cakes dunked into my tea. It definitely helped distract me.

I finally went up to bed well after midnight and have kept the bathroom light on ever since. I am still too creeped out to sleep.

New resolutions...

I WILL ONLY WATCH FEEL GOOD FILMS

I WILL ONLY WATCH THINGS THAT MAKE ME HAPPY

I WILL CHOOSE THE FILMS WE WATCH

I WILL NEVER LET SASKIA CHOOSE ANOTHER FILM TO WATCH WITH ME. EVER!

Friday 3rd April

Strangely slept really well. That surprised me!

Woke up saying my affirmations and looking at my resolutions. There's a lot to remember. Couldn't switch my monkey mind off today to meditate and my attempt at praying was futile: they kept re-bounding off the walls of my brain. Don't know if it was the film or the toxins I poured into my body after 11 p.m, but I just feel meh.

Really doubting myself today. Losing that chapter yesterday knocked the enthusiasm out of me. There are so many doubts and fears kicking around in my head. Want to fight them, but it's so hard. They feel so overwhelming.

I went for a woods walk and called Rosa.

'Whatsup?' (thank you God that she picks up the phone).

'I feel so lost right now. First all that work I built up before this lockdown has gone and then yesterday I lost a big chunk of the novel I was working on, because I'm a techno idiot. Now I have to start even further back. I miss the kids; miss my old life. It all just feels so wrong.' I was in a really grumpy and moaning mood.

'Okay. Stop living in the lack,' she replied (slightly exasperated I noted, since we had a similar conversation a few days earlier).

'I can't help it!'

'Yes you can. It's a choice. You have to *decide* not to think lack thoughts.'

I was quiet. I knew she was right, but I also didn't want to hear her say it. My lack feelings were almost comforting. I knew this place like an old comfy pair of worn slippers.

'Penny? What are you thinking? I can hear you thinking,' she questioned with a laugh.
'It's just, it's just...'

'What? What is it just?'

'What if I am not who you say I am? Who I think I could be? What if I am not that person?' I blurted out almost in tears.

'Ah! I see. So you want to be wallowing in *what if* land then yeah? Want to stay in that comfortable feeling of lack mentality? Is that what you want, to stay ordinary? To not achieve your goals, your dreams or your God-given purpose?'

Ouch. That hurt. How does she manage to do that, to get right into the wound and twist the knife in?

'No. Yes. Er...no.'

'What is it? No or yes? You decide and when you know, call me back.'

Then she hung up the phone. Oh great. Now I've peed her off and lost my main 'go-to' friend. I was skulking on my walk after she ended the call, my head down and kicking at the stones on the ground. My feet kept walking without the engagement of my consciousness, until I found myself along a path of the woods I hadn't taken before. I felt a presence and looked up and then around me. My first fleeting thought was fear as I realised I was in unfamiliar territory. Then a sense of calm washed over me. Something caught my eye. I walked to the bank of trees on the right hand side of the path, where a small crowd of them huddled, intertwined and twisted over one another. It was difficult to see where one tree began and another ended. Intrigued, I moved in for a closer look and found myself staring at a cut out, laminated notecard swinging from a branch of one of the trees. It was hanging from a red and white piece of thick string. The note was cut into the shape of a love heart and the string had been threaded through a little hole at the top. It hung there, owning its space and swaying gently in the fresh, light, spring breeze.

I stepped up closer and held it in my hand. There were three words written in black ink onto the laminated, yellow coloured paper. Someone had taken the time to colour in the paper with a pencil: a child perhaps? But the writing wasn't like that of a young child. The words inscribed simply said,

'Believe in miracles'

I called Rosa straight back. 'I believe in me.' I said, informing her of the note and walking off path and the significance of that moment. She laughed and told me that sometimes our prayers are answered in the most unexpected of ways. She was right, because after she had hung up on our earlier call, I had put up a desperate quick prayer for guidance.

I felt such a sense of peace when I thanked Rosa for her wisdom, then said goodbye and ended the call. I can't remember the walk home or how long it took, but I think I skipped it. And I definitely felt I had a knowing smile etched onto my face.

When I got home, S was awake. She needed a hug. Her and her boyfriend had argued again. I didn't lecture, or preach; I simply hugged her for the longest time.

Then we made some brunch, switched on *Moana*, laughed and sung our favourites from the film and the world seemed to slot straight back into it's happy place.

Sunday 5th April

My period arrived. Now that explains a lot!

Today has been about pigging on chocolate, crisps, chips from the local kebab shop (still open...yesssss!) and half a bottle of wine. Some days you just gotta roll with it. Though I am concerned that if I carry on eating and drinking like this, I will literally be rolling out of this lockdown!

Diary, I saw a funny article online earlier. Cracked me up and was just what I needed after the past few challenging days.

Apparently last month Amazon declared that due to the pandemic, they would only be delivering out essential items and not the non-essential ones like Ninendos and dildos (I know!). Though they still were apparently slipping through the warehouse and into the recipient's hands (haha). Seems the demand for sex toys has increased since the lockdown began. No shit! I then continued reading. The article mentioned how New York's Health Department prepared a guide on how to have safe sex during Corona times. It concluded '*You are your safest sex partner.*'

Now let me get my head around that for one moment. *You are your safest sex partner...* really? What has the world come to when top world health departments have to declare that having a little fiddle with yourself, is the safest way to release any sexual desires right now: during a global pandemic?

So based on that then, dildos and sex toys are definitely essential for a healthy sex life right? I mean if you have those desires, then unless you have truly magical fingers, you may need a little help in that department (talking women here of course). And if copulation with a partner not living with you, is declared a serious danger to one's health, then for the good of all mankind, surely these adult toys are pretty essential right now, given that the human race's survival relies on copulation? Gotta keep the practise up right? Can't go rusty in that department, or humanity will really be in trouble.

So then, if having sex by oneself is the safest sex to have, how come we have an Amazon worker come out and declare that dildos are non-essential items and should be kept on the warehouse shelves? It's bonkers (sorry about the pun, again). I don't know Diary, the whole world has gone crazy in just a couple of weeks.

Why do I get the feeling that the next few months are going to end up being like this? One hand saying this and the other saying that? Oh I just saw another pun in that - definitely a hand job! Okay, now I am cracking up and laughing hysterically at my own jokes and I have only been in lockdown for a little over a week. Hate that laughing really brings attention to my pelvic floor weakness. Must start those kegel exercises. This is getting ridiculous!

I am so never having any more kids! I'm pretty sure that neither my pelvic floor, my flappy tummy, my varicose veins and *especially* my sanity, could cope. Oh Lordy, the thought of getting pregnant again, I'll never sleep. Need some new affirmations:

MY EGGS HAVE ALL GONE
MY WOMB IS ZIPPED SHUT
I AM NOT A BABY MAKING MACHINE
I AM NEVER, EVER HAVING ANY MORE KIDS

Stressed just thinking about it. Though I shouldn't stress since there isn't a man around to tempt me and not sure when there ever will be! At least they are encouraging self practise!

Talking of which, where the heck is my BOB?

Tuesday 7th April

12.45 p.m.

Had a really embarrassing moment this morning. My new addiction to toffees has finally gotten me into trouble. I had just popped one into my mouth at the end of queuing to get into the supermarket. Just as I was about to enter, someone I knew walked out and we both said hi and out of habit, automatically went in to give each other a hug, but of course, quickly pulled away, remembering hugs are not allowed. This in turn caused me to laugh nervously, which lodged the toffee down my throat. Intense spluttering and coughing ensued, which caused everyone around to give me the widest berth. My friend scarpered more out of pure embarrassment at knowing me than anything else (must remember that when all this is over!)

There I stood, choking and coughing on a now un-lodged toffee wedged into the side of my mouth, whilst also surreptitiously crossing my legs for fear of wee pouring down them. I WAS MORTIFIED!

Yet I really did need milk and butter, so after recovering enough for them not to call an ambulance to whisk me away, I walked into the shop. I was trying to be as cool and natural as I could, but knew that I still needed to cough, since the sweet, toffee juice was trickling down my throat and creating a tickle which I really needed to have a huge coughing fit to get rid of. Of course, the very last thing you can do during a pandemic where the first sign of the virus, is a cough, is actually cough. Especially in a supermarket! So not only was I holding my pelvic floor internally, but I was also red faced because of holding in this awful, tickly cough. I grabbed the milk and butter as fast as my contorted body could muster and rushed to the till, paid, then left. As soon as I was out of ear and eye-shot, I coughed my bloody heart out, whilst simultaneously crossing my legs without actually holding a hand to my downstairs, which I really should have done, since my leg crossing job wasn't that effective! Small mercies, that I was wearing black leggings and a long jumper and my car was literally a few minutes walk away. Damn toffee!

8.30 p.m.

I'm missing my kids ☹. Over two weeks now and surpassed the longest time I've been without them. I know they are safe and I speak to them all the time, but for the past eighteen years I've been a mum. I've had part-time and self-employed work, but I've always been there for them. This is really tough for me.

However, it's been lovely to spend quality time with S. We walk every day in the woods around 5 or 6 p.m. and have even watched a few sunsets together. It was tough at first as she has so many teen barriers, but I feel we've started to heal our relationship. I still feel her pain and can't ever appreciate her perspective entirely, but this time together is a gift. And not having the other two here, despite missing them deeply, means there are no distractions for us. I give S space and I have time to write until she wakes up.

This unexpected period in our lives is both a blessing and a wound. I have lost so much, but also immensely gained so much more.

But...thank goodness for gin!!!

Thursday 9th April

I thought I would be really struggling on my own by now. I know it's only been less than three weeks so I haven't given it time yet to really feel any kind of lack other than for my children being home. But, I don't miss the commutes to London. I don't miss the effort of trying. I don't miss wondering if I will get work, or whether I will meet Mr Right on a train, in a coffee shop or on a dating site. I am not really missing seeing many people either. I guess I will if this goes on much longer though. There was talk of another month. I'm not thinking about it. Deliberately.

I have stopped watching the news or reading the headlines. My world has shrunk to a daily morning routine of training my mind to think positively and taking myself into a place of inner peace and calm with meditation and gratitude focus. Miraculously it is working, as I'm able to focus on the information to input into writing. I really do feel more at peace these days and I'm giving off more of a positive and loving vibe. Not that anyone other than S is getting the benefit of those feel-good vibes right now, but I'm banking them up for the benefit of others at a later stage.
Yep, I've definitely gone full out 'woo woo'!

I've also finally written an ingredients list of my perfect partner. I made a new friendship with a life coach woman I've met in a group on social media. We were talking about writing a 'soul mate list' and she told me to make sure I put the penis size down too. That made me laugh so hard (tee hee), as I hadn't thought it was important. She said she once made the mistake of manifesting Mr Perfect with a less than perfect member.

Mmm, I wonder what a perfect size for me would be? Think I'll need a glass of rum for this one...

<u>12.40 a.m.</u>

Finished my list. Oh boy, if this guy does exist, he sure isn't going to be single. No woman in her right mind would let him go. Maybe I should be less fussy on certain aspects? Or at least be a bit more flexible on one of the requirements? Mind you, I have had three big babies. Think I'll keep that one in there just in case it's a game changer. Oh to have the choice Diary!

Friday 10th April

Three weeks tomorrow without the kids. That's so weird. Really missing them. They are coming to visit on Sunday for a couple of hours since S hasn't got the virus. She's on her second tonsillitis infection but no virus. Phew! The kid was a wreck coming back to me. She's looking so much better thank goodness and the healing of our relationship is coming along nicely. As my friend used to say about any relationship that needed healing,

'I will restore to you the years the locusts have eaten.' I think it was the Big G who said it, though my friend also said it a lot.

As long as I don't mention anything to do with her boyfriend, her living situation, the past, her trauma, her weight, my weight, eating dairy, her friends or anything that might create friction, we're good. The hardest part is finding something I can talk about!

The weather is so lovely at present and I'm so enjoying writing on the chair by the window in the living room. The sun pours through from mid morning to mid afternoon. Since I have uninterrupted peace until at least midday, I can write up to five thousand words a day.

Apparently, it's the Easter holidays and therefore no school, so Lily doesn't call until after noon, Saskia stays in bed and Ben is apparently in Xbox heaven at his dad's. It's like having an exposed creative freeway to tap into. My morning walks are reflective and if I am not on a call, I have Dr Wayne Dyer speaking wisdom from the Audible app in my headphones.

Life feels good right, now despite everything.

Though I do wish I had someone special in my life: a guy to message or flirt with, or someone to let me know they are thinking of me. Perhaps when this is all over, I might actually be open to meeting a guy? And also not keep attracting the types of players I do. Which reminds me...bloody idiot that publishing director ended up being!

Mind you, despite not seeing anyone, I can still pull! My 25-year-old postman seems to have taken a shine to me. How funny. You still got it girl ;-)

Sunday 11th April

10.30 a.m.

I had the weirdest dream.

It involved the actors Brad Pitt and Chris Pine. Both asked me to marry them and I had to choose. What a dilemma! I woke up sweating. Not out of sexual pleasure or anything, but because in my dream I had to decide if I wanted to be called Penelope Pitt or Penelope Pine. What's with the P's? And it's worse if I double barrelled. Can you imagine? Penelope Wood-Pine, or Penelope Wood-Pitt? Talk about out of the fire and into the frying pan. Ok now I can't stop laughing. Penelope Wood-Pine. Penelope Pine-Wood. Wood-Pitt! Oh my. I have tears rolling down my face. This will keep me going all day. Wood-Pitt...

It took me a while to properly wake up today, since I seemed to be stuck in that awakening dream and unable to shake it off. I was trying to imagine what celebrity I could substitute for either Brad or Chris, that had a surname that would either go with my first name or at least make my name sound slightly more exotic and less like sitting around a campfire! I couldn't. Why did Brad have to have Pitt as his surname?

Jenna...Carly...Sarah...Daisy...Florence? Oh my gosh, Florence(s)Pitt! Haha, no that definitely wouldn't work - Florence Spitt! Oh how I amuse myself Diary! That's what I spent the first hour of my morning doing. What the heck have I been reduced to? Fantasising about marrying one of the world's top movie stars, whom I will probably never meet, only to be in a quandary over changing my surname. Really? Could that be a deal breaker really? Penelope Pitt. Penelope Wood-Pitt. Penelope Pine-Wood. Yep, seems it really could!

Kids over today. Yay! Catch you later D.

<u>5.30 p.m.</u>

It may only have been for a couple of hours, but it was so bloody good to see the kids earlier. I've missed them so much! S went for a walk with her dad and I went out into the fields with the kids. They are so lovely. I'm so proud of them. I do worry about how they will cope coming back to live in this wee, cramped house after staying at their dad's grander place for so long. I know that's crazy Diary as my kids aren't like that, but I did have great plans for our future home and now who's to say when that will happen?

I must start my affirmations again and not allow what's happened to attack my dreams. Who knows what path my life will take after this book is published? I must remain positive. I MUST REMAIN POSITIVE! Will say these three affirmations all day every day –

I AM RICH

I AM SUCCESSFUL

I AM ACHIEVING MY DREAMS

<u>9.20 p.m.</u>

The affirmations didn't help this evening. When the kids left earlier, I took myself up into the bathroom and sobbed. S was in the garden shouting at her boyfriend. I thought they were back on again, but the way she is screaming at him, I'm not so sure. I'm feeling the lack right now: of the kids, of my work, of my dreams, of a partner that doesn't yet exist and of direction. This is probably one of the first days where I have felt real despair since all this began.

I started gin o'cocktail before 6 p.m. today. That's naughty too. I wish I was better at my resolutions and actually stuck to them. Already had two and they were pretty strong. At this rate, I'll be on a bottle of gin a week. It took me over three years to get through the last bottle I had before lockdown! Who have I become, a Gin Lush Queen?

1.45 a.m.
I'm sloshed. Slossssshhhhhheddddd. Haha. I Facetimed Ed, from Louisiana at

1 a.m. and we got so tipsy together. It was so funny; he's hilarious. He was drinking straight whisky and I'd already been drinking since before six, so I was really giggly and naughty. He's six hours behind me so he was even naughtier than me for drinking so early. Haha.

We talked dating sites, sex and little dinkies. So funny! So going to put 'big dinky' on my perfect man list now. No question about it! Hah. Can't stop giggling to myself. Oh my goodness, it's almost 2 a.m. on a Monday morning! Mega naughty.

Soooo tired.

Wood-Pitt...it's still cracking me up! Must stop in case anyone hears. S is actually asleep before me for a change, blimey.

Wood-Pine. Hah! Okay, definitely going to stop keeping myself awake laughing. Oh but it's so good to laugh! Wonder if Brad will let me just keep my own name? That would be so much easier and solve a lot of the problems.

Am I really writing that? I mean, really? Have I so lost the plot (or so drunk) that I have come to the conclusion that Brad is going to marry me and because I don't want to have a weird surname that I get to keep my own? What the heck is wrong with me? It's only been a few weeks and I am now certifiably mad. There's no hope for me. Only one thing left to do then...

Time to dream about Brad ;-)

Monday 12ᵗʰ April

Routines all out of sync today. Bleeding hangover from hell. And I woke up at crazy o'clock, with the first crack of sunlight stabbing through my ineffective curtains and found it virtually impossible to get back to sleep. Damn my body clock! Couldn't write either so watched films all day with S. Went for a walk with her in the afternoon and at last she opened up to me. So sad for her struggling with issues, but really can see this time with her as a blessing. So many kids must be struggling with what's going on right now? Hope it doesn't last so we can all get back to where we were before, or perhaps not exactly the same. Seems God really knew what he was doing to bring her to me exactly at the right time and at the start of lockdown. Amazing really.

My book is a third the way through and that couldn't have happened if the kids were here. When I look back at this time, I will see the pattern of how everything happens for a reason. What that reason is, I am not sure, but I know this time with S is a blessing for us both. She's such a beautiful soul. I feel very blessed to have what I do. I mustn't compare myself to others so much and be more grateful for all I do have, especially right now when the world is in such disarray and so many people are suffering and struggling. Rosa keeps reminding me not to live in a lack mentality. It's so hard, but I know my situation could always be a lot worse.

Time to make some new resolutions! Don't care that it's not New Year. I need to get a grip!

1. I will NOT drink more than one glass of anything alcoholic mid week

2. I will try NOT to drink mid week but NOT be too hard on myself if I do, but it must only be ONE glass of something

3. I will NOT drink before 6 p.m. any night of the week

4. I will only think POSITIVE thoughts

5. I will NOT think of the things I don't have and only be grateful for the things I do
6. I will have the best body at the end of this lockdown

7. I will positively manifest what I want and not kick myself for not yet having the things I want that I don't yet have
8. I will tell myself I am the BEST MOTHER and not beat myself up for not being the best mother I can be

9. I will look at my ideal soul mate list every night before I go to bed and manifest the heck out of it so I do not ever end up in another situation like this with just my face to look at every flipping day (got carried away there sorry)

10. Tell myself I am AMAZING every morning that I am blessed to wake up and every night before I go to bed

11. Get eight hours sleep and go to bed by 10.30 p.m. every night.

12. I will NOT eat a bag of M&S toffees every 3 days

Wednesday 14th April

Had a really stressful day. Went to bed at gone midnight, started drinking before 6 p.m. and only wrote 350 words. S and her boyfriend screaming at each other all day and the news feeds are talking about the lockdown going on until May. Some days are good and some days are a shitfest. Today was the latter.

Not sure how many of my mid-year resolutions I broke today, but I think it was pretty much most of them. I didn't drink yesterday though!!

Called David because I am a masochist and needed to hear the words '*Get back on the flipping train Penny*'. He obliged.

I'm on the train. I'm not getting off. I may be stuck on a train not knowing where I am going and it may feel like it's broken down or has a points failure (don't they always?) but I won't get off.

There's always tomorrow. I'll start life again tomorrow. Thank buggery flip for tomorrow.

Friday 16th April

I keep having weird dreams and last night's was pretty surreal to say the least.

I was lying on a sunbed besides a pool on holiday somewhere. I was by myself. And completely stark naked, except I seemed oblivious to this fact. I got up to go for a swim in the pool, when everyone started pointing and laughing. I didn't understand why, until I looked down. There attached to my groin, was the biggest penis I have ever seen in my life. And it was apparently mine. I had boobs too, so I wasn't a man.

I woke up in a sweat and the first thing I did was check under my PJ bottoms. Yep, no tickle tackle. Phew. But how bizarre?

Perhaps I should stop checking my soul mate list before going to bed at night? I had underlined 'Big dinky' three times. It's obviously made a huge impression on my sub conscious mind!

I called Andy my music producer friend. Randy Andy would love that dream.

'You're sexually frustrated girl. You need to get some action!' he piped up.

'Andy we're in lockdown for one and I have my daughter with me for two. Plus, let's face it, I've hardly got ripe pickings going on just now!'

'It doesn't stop me.'

'What? But it's lockdown. How can you? You can't can you?'

'Just saying...'

'Go on. Spill the beans. You can't just say that and leave it there. What you been up to?'

He then went on to tell me about this younger woman who served him at the supermarket. How he used his charm on her and managed to persuade her to come back to his a few times over the past two weeks.

I was horrified. Then questioned myself over my reaction. Why do I feel so strongly about it? This is Andy after all - the guy who videoed himself having a threesome with a Russian model and her mate and wanted to send it to me. I said no of course!

'Get out and get some action Pen. Be a rebel' he said before having to rush off to a business conference call.

I thought about it, for just a brief moment. Could I really have illicit sex during a lockdown, or any time really, could I?

The thought remained with me all day. I called David. He was good with this type of thing.

'No you wouldn't and couldn't. One you can't so it isn't going to happen and two, you aren't like that. It's just not who you are. So get rid of that thought and get on with your writing. Sex is a distraction. Go find BOB and get back on the train woman.'

I agreed with him of course and went back to writing about Sylvia, a woman who finds out in her thirties that she's the product of her mother's illicit affair with a married man. The man who she called father her entire life, was an alcoholic abuser who died from drink driving when Sylvia was in her teens, but not before he left a cruel legacy of self destruction and low self worth on his family. The realisation that she had a different father to her siblings, explained so much about her childhood feelings of not fitting into the family. It also sent Sylvia into free fall. A period of self destructive, learned behaviours followed, as well as a string of insecure and dead-end relationships. Then, after an encounter with a spiritual woman, she began a search to find her real father and to finally cut herself free away from a brother and sister who tormented her throughout her entire life. Their mother died from cancer when Sylvia was just twenty-two, so the search for her birth father was made all the more complex and compounding.

My thoughts turned to Sylvia's mother and the affair that led to the extra marital conception of Sylvia. What drove her mother, petrified of her abusive husband, to embark on such a wild adventure? I mean, the risks involved were immense! Her husband could have killed her if he found out. And then to discover that she was pregnant with this man's child...what thoughts were going through her head? And why did she not stay with this man and leave her husband? Why indeed. That's precisely the part I am now writing.

So it was quite apt to have the two conversations today with Andy and David and to have both sides of the coin shown to me. We have a choice in our lives; we always have a choice.

So right now, I choose not to jump into the sack with a man just to satisfy a sexual urge. I choose to stay safe and to remain single at this weird time.

Besides there are two overriding factors that contribute to this decision –

a)   There isn't any guy to have illicit sex with

b)   I rarely O anyway, so what's the point?

I must write this into the book somewhere. The O thing is definitely worth exploring...

Wow D. I tell you so much. Hope nobody ever reads my diary.

Saturday 17ᵗʰ April

Kids are here tomorrow all day. Yay! They're back to homeschooling with their dad on Monday. I have been so blessed not to have to do that. I could never have started writing with them living here. My house is so tiny with no escape places and Ben doesn't stop talking: all day everyday, unless he is shouting at someone through his headset on Xbox. It's so tiring listening to him as he plays that damn Fortnite game and no matter how many times he is told to turn down the noise, he continues reverberating the house with his 'What?' 'Why did you do that?' 'This is so stupid!' and 'I hate this game.'

He doesn't hate it enough to save our poor ears from having to listen to him playing the damn thing all the bleeding time though.

It's been quite lonely at home to be honest. When S isn't sleeping, she's on her phone. Who the heck does she talk to all day and all night? If she isn't talking loudly to her boyfriend (they are off and on every single day), or one of her friends, she's practising her make up or braiding her hair in front of the living room mirror listening to that Tiger King programme on

Netflix. I try not to listen, I really do, but it's impossible given our small living space. Carol Baskin definitely did it right? What a horrible man that weird Tiger King guy is. Ugh. I really am not watching it, but when it's in my face, I can't help but get suckered in! I once stood over Saskia's shoulder listening for the whole episode, whilst holding a tea towel in one hand and a dish I had just dried in the other. That's how addictive the damn programme is. If I knew I was going to watch it, I would've sat down!

Called Jenni. So good to hear someone having an even more challenging life than me, which sounds awful I know. At least I have S at home; Jenni has no one bless her. Mind you, she does seem to be off her head most times I call her, so I'm not sure if her life is that awful compared to mine, or flipping amazing, depending on the perspective!

At 8 p.m. I did something I had never done before - I joined a zoom party. I was invited by somebody from a new Facebook group I join a couple of weeks ago. I was so excited to be making new friends and even dressed up as though I were going on a night out. S made me one of her delicious cocktails – with rum this time and even curled my hair. We had a laugh getting me ready and I can honestly say, that this was the best part of the whole evening. There I was all ready to chat, giggle and feel like I wasn't stuck at home in a lockdown situation, but alas, I was so disappointed. This group had obviously been going for quite a while and probably well before March, as they all bantered between each other and used first names like they'd been best mates since birth. Whilst Billy no mates here, sat with the same drink for twenty minutes, smiling, nodding and silent, waiting for someone to say hi or ask me my name. But it didn't come. I felt like one of those friends invited only to make up the numbers.

54

I disappeared after twenty-three minutes. S asked how it went. I lied and told her that I got bored and that I would rather have tea and cake and watch *Moana* with her. So that's what we did. I put on my PJs and we made a Victoria Sponge cake and flipped on our favourite film. Cos that's how we roll in the Woods family!

11.45 p.m.

I haven't once made it to bed once before midnight yet. I think I have broken almost all my resolutions so far and some I habitually break. I'm the world's worse at being committed to my resolutions. So I've written some new additions for my resolution wall:

I WILL NOT BREAK MY RESOLUTIONS
I WILL COMMIT TO MY RESOLUTIONS
STICK TO YOUR FLIPPING RESOLUTIONS!

Must try harder. Tomorrow. I'll definitely try harder tomorrow.

Tuesday 21st April

11.30 p.m.

Now this is interesting D. Getting a lot of messages from single male friends and male connections talking about how much they are missing sex. Seeing it on posts too. Many say it's the longest they've gone without having it. Mmm.

So, let's backtrack a bit here. I have been on various dating sites over the past two years and when you ask a guy when was the last time they were in a relationship or dating, a lot of them reply with stuff like, 'Last year sometime' or 'about six months ago' or something similar to that. Many men I have met, spoken to or messaged, gave the impression that they hadn't been with a woman since their last girlfriend, which was usually months ago, and that they don't engage in casual sex. What a fool you have been Penny!

Seems men are far more truthful right now and many are finally admitting that six weeks is the longest they have been without sex for a very long time and that they are pretty desperate. I think one guy used the words 'gagging for it'. Another said he was so desperate he could 'shag a sheep'. I think I was meant to find that offensive being Welsh, but I just laughed it off.

Back to the desperate for sex thing - now the thing is, the maths don't quite work out for me on that one. Does that mean the guys I met and spoke to prior to lockdown weren't telling the truth? Blimey. Either I am very naïve or they are damn good at pulling the wool of my/women's eyes? Wool...back to sheep again? Maybe it's because men are baaa...stards? Hah. I am tipsy Diary, what do you expect?

Really good to know though, just in case I ever decide to date again, which at this point, looks highly unlikely given the state of the world, my inability to find a decent guy and that probably any single guy coming out of lockdown will be like a puppy humping a trouser leg – big desires and just about anything will do!

Anyway, apart from feeling lonely and wanting a hug and support from a partner, I don't feel like I am particularly missing much right now. Whether I will feel like that in another month or so, who knows? I've been single long enough for it not to make any difference to me anyway. Saying that, I might be horny as hell by the time we get let out of our caves.

Best I stay off the rum until then, just to be sure. And if I get those urges, there is always, the elusive BOB. Just got to find where I last put it. Damn!

Friday 24th April

I had the strangest conversation with Andy today. OMG did I embarrass myself!

Andy – 'I think I have Corona'

Me – 'Really? Why, what are your symptoms?'

Andy – 'Tickly cough, feel tired, loss of taste and smell.'

Me – 'Oh no. Sounds like the virus alright. You feeling okay though? '

Andy – 'Yes, I'm fine. Think it's a mild version as I've had it a few days now and it hasn't got any worse.'

Me – 'Do you know how you caught it?'

Andy – (coughs nervously but it could just be the 'rona) 'Eliana'.

Me – 'What is that? A supermarket place near you?'

Andy laughs. Doesn't stop for ages. Then coughs. 'No silly! Eliana the Russian model!'

Me – 'Oh the threesome girl?"

Andy – 'Er no, her friend. The other girl was Tatiana.'

Me – 'Right...'

Andy – 'I got caught out. She came with a cough. I should have known better.'

Me – 'Is that a thing? Can you do that?'

Andy – 'Do what?'

Me – 'Come with a cough? I've coughed and farted at the same time before, but never come whilst coughing.'

The sounds of Andy laughing ring through my ears. His laughter induces his coughing, which induces his laughing. It was taking a while. Finally I ask what was so funny, thinking it might be my use of the word 'farted', since I am rarely crude like that with him.

Andy – 'Oh Pen, you're a card. That's why I love talking to you. No you idiot. I don't think that's actually a *thing* by the way, but I might be wrong. What I meant, was that Eliana ARRIVED with a cough when I met her.'

Me – 'Oh...! well what else could I say?

Andy – 'I have to go. I've another conference call. Oh I love that...'came with a cough'...'coughed and farted at the same time'...haha!'

I could hear his laughter ringing in my ears long after he put the phone down. How embarrassing. I cringed for a while after the call but did chuckle later telling the story to S (she is eighteen after all). She looked at me as if I had grown two heads, then said something about being 'as dull as a brush'. I guess I can sometimes be a little bit naïve.

Monday 27th April

The sun was out today. The weather is so beautiful right now. I love sitting outside the front door when I return from my woods walk. I make porridge and listen to the birds chirping away (acceptable at this time of day since they've already woken me up hours ago!)

I love the way my neighbours are all busying themselves outside their houses. One is sorting out their garage (I've been gifted a couple of outside chairs and a lamp so far). The guy two doors up from us, seems to get a thrill out of washing his car - three times this week (bit obsessive I think, given he hasn't driven it once since lockdown started). The woman across the street is busy doing her front garden, planting bulbs and doing other gardening things I know very little about. Can't be good at everything right? Maybe one day I'll discover my green fingers, but until then, those fingers are busy in lots of other creative pies. My brain suddenly switched to thinking of a naked Brad Pitt. Now how did that happen? Reminder to self – Penelope Wood-Pitt!

Cul-de-sac living is a weird thing I have discovered. It's probably the first time in the two years of living here, that most of my neighbours have said hello. I always envisaged that being in a cul-de-sac, was like living amongst lots of friendly, 'can I borrow some sugar?' neighbours, all rallying round each other, chatting over the garden fence and stringing out bunting for street parties. Such an idyllic life in my head of what we would be encountering when we moved here. That's certainly how I sold it to my three when we moved in. Alas, there aren't any kids nearby and poor Ben is the youngest around us. In fact, I think I'm the youngest around here! Lily disliked being here so much to begin with, that she called it 'cull the oldies'. Not very nice, but I did see the funny side.

I don't find my noisy neighbour's barking dog funny though. Must write new affirmations:

I DO LOVE MY NEIGHBOURS
EVEN THEIR BLOODY YAPPY DOG

Damn. I can hear them shouting at each other again. I'm really trying to think positive thoughts about them Diary, I really am. But I do wish they would shut up!

Maybe it's time to start meditating in the evening also? That'll distract me. Ah. They've closed their door. Bliss.
'Shall I start the dinner mum?' S calls out from the kitchen when I return inside from writing. 'Glass of wine?"

My life is sooooo good right now!

I'll start meditating tomorrow.

Sunday 3rd May

I've written sixty-three thousand words so far. I'm over two-thirds the way to finishing my first novel. Yes! My plan is to get to eighty thousand as a target minimum. The rate I am going, I will get there in the next week or so. Who'd have thought?

I feel very proud of myself. It's so strange how life works out. On one hand I have lost so much and on the other, I am realising lifelong, childhood dreams. The weather is amazing and I have a tan coming and it's only the beginning of May. Fabulicious! I have even started doing yoga followed by press-ups and sit-ups. Writing hasn't been quite as kind on my body as my mind. I tried to put on a dress yesterday, that I wore just three months ago, and I look like a jumbo sausage squeezing itself into a tiny slinky toy. It wasn't a good look.

Wow! How could I have put on so much weight in such a small amount of time? I blame the crisps, the sweets, the bars of Lindt chocolate I keep buying for S (it's her favourite), but that I keep sneakily eating so have to keep replacing (and then eating and replacing...), the rich foods she cooks late in the evening and the copious amounts of alcohol I seem to be drinking every flipping night! My body now knows when it's gin o'clock. It starts doing a holiday dance. I down my laptop, blast some music and start jigging around the living room. S is used to this by now and just rolls her eyes and leaves me to it. At what stage do I tell myself that I am not actually on holiday? I just know that things will dramatically change when the other two return home, so it's like my sub conscious mind is saying 'Party on now love; get it whilst you can!'

Tried doing the Joe Wicks exercising thing for three days straight, but I couldn't walk properly for almost a week afterwards, so I decided to give up. Hats off for anyone continuing with his workouts though. I love how he has encouraged kids and parents to exercise together and he's getting so many people off their building backsides. Shame I couldn't bear the pain since my backside has definitely built up! Plus he's quite cute in an, 'if I was thirty again' kinda way. *If I was thirty?* Argh. When did I become this old?

Amazing that I have now finished a bottle of gin, 2 bottles of wine and half a bottle of brandy. And it's only been six weeks of lockdown. Perhaps it's time to stop thinking of this as a holiday? Never drunk so much on a regular basis in my entire life! I wonder what Joe Wickes would make of my unhealthy alcohol, crisps and sugar addictions??

Back to my resolutions I think. Damn, where did I put them? I took them off the wall in frustration the other night and hid them someplace. I was a bit tipsy. Great hiding place though as no matter where I've looked, I can't find them!

I remember the one that said I mustn't drink every day. Or was it only one glass of something a day? Must find it and start again. And try to do at least more than one day's worth this time. Damn this lockdown. When I come out of this, I will have a red nose, an even flabbier tummy and a pickled liver to boot ☹.

Monday 4ᵗʰ May

It's so beautiful and hot today. This is bliss. Day whatever of lockdown and it really feels like a holiday today. Now on seventy thousand words. It's all made so much easier with the glorious sunshine. Lily is happy because she is sunbathing at her dad's. Ben is happy since he's had no school over the Easter break. According to Lily, he's apparently a nightmare to get to do anything remotely connected to school and his dad is having to constantly coerce him to sit down and do something school related. Lily tells me everyday how much she and Ben hate online schoolwork. I am absolutely dreading taking over in the homeschooling department, especially in this teeny house. I am under no illusions - it's going to be living hell.

Until they return, I am going to keep writing, doing my daily routines, spending time with S in the afternoon/evenings and trying to keep a positive mindset. The sun is shining and life, at least on paper, is pretty okay to be honest.

And yet...I still feel the lack in my life. I feel very lonely at times and I miss socialising and being work busy. I miss my friends and miss banter and adult conversations. I miss going on dates with the hope that finally the guy I am meeting might just be 'the one' (they never are). I miss sitting in my favourite coffee shop and flirting with that guy I quite fancy. I also miss Richard, which is crazy as we split up fifteen months ago and he turned out to be a right pig! But that's lockdown for you, getting you to miss any human connection!

I tell you what I don't miss though – queuing for just about everything. It drives me insane! We are always running out of something or other here, so I am in the long supermarket queue most days! My life has become being at home, walking in the woods and standing in supermarket queues. I could arrange a delivery of course, but apart from the apparent lack of delivery slots, I feel it's only fair to leave them to the elderly and vulnerable and who can't or shouldn't be out shopping. I'm fit and healthy and never even get the flu, so as long as I stay safe and not go touching women's skirts buying avocados, I should be fine!

To think I used to enjoy going to the supermarket and sometimes even hung around the reduced goods section in the evening, in case I met a guy. I have found that single men on their way home from work, seem to go for the reduced food if shopping early in the evening. I did try mooching around the meat section once, but as a non-meat eater, it made me feel quite nauseous, which isn't the best look for pulling!

Anyway, whoever said that the supermarket is a great place to meet a guy, never went to mine! Not that I have to worry about that anymore, flirting in supermarkets these days can get you arrested. Breathing anywhere close to the opposite sex might get you barred and unless the guy is into eyes only (which would really concern me to be honest), then I think it can be said, that supermarket hook ups are something that happened to other people, in another time, place and no Corona dimension!

Mostly though, I miss normality. Will that ever return and will we remember the benefits of being in lockdown when we return to our old lives and routines? Time will tell.

However, I will not miss being addicted to M&S toffees, but that's on a whole different level! Must slow down though, as dentists are also closed I think? I will not however, miss that damned barking dog next door when I am trying to have a kip whilst S is cooking me dinner.

My kids want a dog. I am never getting a flipping dog!!!

Tuesday 12th May

It's such a beautiful, hot day. So blessed to be able to relax in the sun instead of homeschooling. Mind you, the kids right now have a big garden and a hot tub, so they have it pretty good where they are. Would so love to be on a beach somewhere: Spain or Greece would be ideal. Oh how I'd love to be on holiday, in a pool, floating on a lilo, with the sun beaming onto my bikini clad body. Right now though, I'd settle for a hot tub!

'Would you like some lunch Mum? Fancy a chicken Caesar salad?'

I turn to look at Saskia hanging out of the living room window with a big smile across her face. I checked my watch (and my heart as I am sure it missed a few beats there). Just after 2 p.m.

'Yes please? I'd love that. Thanks love.'

Diary, who needs a holiday when this feels just like one? Here I am, thinking of nothing at all, with no one around, just me and writing happy thoughts. And lunch getting made for me too. This feels so much what heaven must feel like. Pure bliss!

And then the neighbours start shouting...argh.

Think happy thoughts. Think happy thoughts. Where the hell are my earphones? Will stick on some positive meditation music and drone out their interminable noise. Must do more affirmations. I am getting wound up too quickly and easily. I should be a vessel of peace right now.

They're shouting at each other again. Why does the dad always shout instead of talk? If he didn't shout, the others in the house wouldn't either. I can't bear it; it's driving me insane.

'Shut up!'

'Mum! Are you okay? Did you just tell the neighbours to be quiet?' Saskia pops her head out of the window, looking quite astonished.

''Did I say that aloud? Do you think they heard?'

'Well, they went back inside and slammed the door shut, so I am pretty sure they did...'

'Whoops!' I whisper sheepishly and slink lower into the chair.

'I'm going to start lunch now. Sorry, been on the phone to Alia.'

'No probs. I can wait' what is it with teenagers and their flipping phones? Can't believe I said shut up aloud. How rude of me! Oh well, at least it's quiet now.

<u>11.35 p.m.</u>
I found those resolutions and blue tacked them back up onto my bedroom wall. I'd hidden them under a pile of jumpers in a trunk. I only found them as I was looking for BOB. I thought about putting them up on the kitchen wall, in the space between the alcohol bottles and the snack cupboard, but I don't want S to think I THINK that I have a problem with self control. I KNOW I do, but she doesn't have to know that I think I know I do as well. Blimey that was confusing!

When this is all over, I am on a sugar free, crisp free, alcohol free, diet coke free, chocolate free, cheese free diet. What's happened to me? Where has the healthy me gone? And will she ever return? Will my size 8 clothes ever fit me again, especially as my size 10 might not soon if I keep going the way I am? Will I once again see the line of my caesarean scar under the flap of my belly flab? Not only am I single in lockdown, but the chances of looking hot naked in front of a guy after all this is over, is looking pretty darn slim right now too. Slim? I think not Penelope. I think bloody not! Argh....

Thursday 14th May

I scared myself silly today. I read in a magazine that jumping up and down in front of the mirror naked, will show you where you need to tone up. So, with S apparently asleep and me feeling bad about how everything is starting to feel really snug on me, I stripped down to nothingness and starting jumping up and down, in front of the mirror whilst playing dance music loud. As well as checking the front bits, I was also turning around a few times, to see what my backside bits were doing.

I was horrified! Bits weren't just wobbling, they were flapping! I was doing the 8 o'clock clap on my own at 11.34 a.m., with my body parts and not my hands. My boobs were giving the biggest round of applause and my thighs looked like sails bellowing in a storm. But the biggest shock, was how my mummy tummy flapped up and down over my C Scar. I was so engrossed at watching my body go into flapping jelly mode, that I failed to see S walk into the living room.

'Mum! What the heck are you doing?'

I turned sharply to see my oldest standing there with her hands over her eyes and laughing her head off. She must have seen the whole jump up and flap down thing before alerting me to her presence.

I yelped and darted into the kitchen to hide behind the snack cupboard. Oh the irony!

All I could hear was her laughing and saying she was wetting herself.

'Stop it! I have to get my clothes on!' I managed to yell back. I was mortified, especially as I hadn't groomed my private parts in almost three months.

'Cant...stop...laughing! I'm actually peeing myself!' I peeked my head round the corner to see her crouched on the floor, leaning against the wall, whilst somehow crossing her legs at the same time. Tears were streaming down her face. Then a thought hit me and I suddenly felt sick.

'You didn't film it did you? Please tell me you didn't?'

'No Mum of course I didn't. What do you take me for?'

'Well you film me doing everything else!' It's true. She has countless videos of me laughing, crying, dancing, saying something stupid (often) and so many of my facial expressions whilst watching TV, I could audition for Gogglebox without trying! I apparently have a TV watching face and from what I have seen from her videos, it isn't that attractive a look!

She agrees to go back upstairs (she needed to change apparently) whilst I retrieve my clothes AND my dignity. Will I ever live that moment down with her? I am pretty sure it will come back to literally bite me in my flabby, flapping bum further down the line?

9 p.m.

I considered the image of my body parts slapping away so easily. I tried not to ponder on my daughter seeing the same image. How much this lockdown has changed things, my body included. I think of not having the kids home and only enjoying snatches of time with them, of the friends who can't visit their parents and loved ones, of non cohabiting lovers unable to appreciate comfort from each other, of jobs lost and careers ruined, of long queues and lack of freedom.

That will get better soon right D? We will soon get out and be able to meet people again won't we?

Why the heck am I asking you Diary? I have officially lost the plot. Lockdown has driven me to consulting my Diary for advice.

Must think only positive thoughts. We are all safe and virus free. I have almost finished my book. I have a tan. The weather is fab. And...if I lift up my belly I can still see my C Scar and my downstairs area.

See...life is fab after all!

Friday 15th May

Collected Saskia's things from her digs in London. Chaos! It was all in bags and boxes. It was the first opportunity to do this because of lockdown restrictions. She's been living out of a suitcase for the past 2 months and borrowing from me and her sister (though she hasn't asked). It felt weird to be travelling to London during lockdown. The roads are so quiet. I felt guilty being out, even though this is a necessary trip and it's only the two of us.

Mind you, if I thought our little Surrey town had too many cyclists driving half of the town's population mad and the other to the bike shop, it seems that the whole of the West London population has also bought a damned pushbike. Not quite the easy, mooching drive into London I had anticipated!

My tiny house is full of bags, suitcases and teen paraphernalia. All her clothes need a wash and sorting through. Didn't she ever use the washing machine at her place? So stressed! I absolutely hate having this much clutter in my house and moving always creates so much anxiety in me. I've moved more times than I've had holidays. It's true! I worked it out the other day. Not that I am bored or anything. S is sunbathing in the garden and leaving me to it. I wish I had a fairy godmother right now to tackle this mammoth task for me. I often wish I had a fairy godmother to tackle a lot of things for me to be honest!

It's 3.47 p.m. I'm moving gin o' cocktail forward 2.13 hours! Needs must.

Gone midnight

Bloody knackered. If I never see a piece of clothing again, it'll be too soon. Sooo much washing! I only had the one drink today. I was just too damn tired and I knew I would be asleep on the sofa if I had more. I did however, eat a whole bag of M&S fudge. Won't be buying those again in a hurry. Thought the bag would last longer if I'm being completely honest. I obviously grossly underestimated quite how small the bag was.

We did sit and watch a film together though. That felt good. My choice – a chick flick. S fell asleep saying it wasn't her thing. Apparently she only watches documentaries, paranormal stuff or horror movies. Yep, I know about the horror movies! We are so far removed from each other in our television preferences. Given the world situation, I need laughter and lightness, so chick flick every single time for me. Or Disney. S loves a Disney film and if I put on *Moana*, we are both bellowing out the tunes and smiling like crazy every single time. I think that's definitely our happy film.

Ok, now I am humming 'You're Welcome' to myself. Love that song and his voice. And now I have an image of The Rock's voluptuous pecs in my head. Nice image to go to sleep to though. Mmm. You're welcome...

Sunday 17th May

Ten washes later....

But at least I had the kids this weekend. The weather is so lush. Super warm today. I love being in summer dresses or shorts and vests. At least they still fit. Oh, I could definitely live somewhere hot.

I am almost finished writing my first novel, my kids are all safe and well and nobody I know has had Coronavirus thank goodness. I've got a few ideas for future work options and I'm doing a couple of painting commissions. It's all so promising considering the work I've lost.

I do have to drop the gin o'clock thing though. It's definitely become an interesting habit! As well as the toffees and now fudge. What has happened to me? Who have I become? Who is this person who consumes copious amounts of wine, rum, gin, crisps, toffees, fudge and anything with fat in? Can the woman who hardly ate snacks or drank alcohol come back now please? I'm declaring your holiday break well and truly over!

Oh Lordy Diary, I am definitely becoming even more weird that I was before all this started. I know you know. And writing that makes me even weirder! There's no hope for me, I'm losing the plot! Argh!

Monday 25th May

My book is finished. Yes! *Where there's a will, there's a way* goes the saying. It's been a lifetime of waiting to fulfil that dream. Really hope it's good enough and people like it.

No wait. One thing I really have learned over this lockdown, is that my words create my reality. So I refuse to say 'may' or 'hope' and definitely not 'hope it's good enough'. Darn girl...you change your language to tell the Universe exactly what you expect to happen. Okay...

I AM A SUCCESSFUL AUTHOR

I AM A BRILLIANT WRITER

PEOPLE LOVE MY BOOK

I AM A NUMBER ONE BEST SELLING AUTHOR

Well D, looks like I am really getting into this manifestation and affirmations stuff. It is so going to happen for me, I have just got to keep on believing, which isn't easy since I am the biggest Doubting Thomas I know.

S and I are really relishing our time together. Her skin and body ailments have healed totally. She quit smoking soon after she arrived and hasn't had another since. She looks healthy for the first time in a very long time. She might be costing me a fortune every week in shopping, but I don't mind though. I don't spend money on petrol, coffee shops, clothes, travelling to London, or even alcohol, since so far, most of it has been gifted to me. I see the kids every weekend and do that Facetime thing with them via WhatsApp twice a day. My lockdown body could look better and that jumping up and down thing really put the heeby jeebies up me. Urgh. Can't imagine what I'd look like without my daily walks and exercises to burn a few calories!

I have deliberately slowed down on the drinking now and don't even drink everyday. Wow, that's a vast improvement. It's not the alcohol consumption that concerns me though, but the addiction to toffees! Going through a bag every three days at present! Though nobody's perfect right Diary and if it helps get me through these crazy times, then what's the real harm?

Glad I have you to talk to Diary. You are a great friend.

Did I really just right that? Oh boy!

Wednesday 27ᵗʰ May

Last night S and I watched the film Shirley Valentine. I found it in a pile of DVDs she brought in from the garage, in a box marked 'charity shop'. She chose it for a laugh she said. I'm not sure she found it quite as entertaining as I did.

Diary, watching that film, I had a smack in the face realisation. YOU ARE MY WALL and I am the equivalent of a lockdown Shirley Valentine discovering who she is! Okay, Shirley and I are not quite the same; in fact, there are very few similarities, but her talking to the wall out of loneliness and desperation, is exactly like me writing in my diary. What have I become, talking to my diary and telling it all my secrets? The wall didn't answer Shirley Valentine either Diary, so no pressure when I'm asking you for advice! Okay, even writing that makes me feel like I *am* bloody Shirley Valentine!

It made me wonder if anyone is ever going to be kissing my stretch marks after this? I know they've increased, as both S and I can now testify after my mortifying mirror flapping escapade! Still, if Shirley could pull a hunk like Costas and get him to kiss her lower parts, then I am sure there's a guy out there willing to kiss mine? Though I'd prefer him not to have to lift up my tummy flab in order to find them first! Mmm, must lose this extra weight before we come out of lockdown, just in case I do meet Mr Right For Me. Perhaps I should listen to the kids and get a dog? They do say that dog walking is a great way to find a partner. Mmm, now that's food for thought.

Which makes me wonder how people are going to be able to date again if we always have to social distance and wear masks? Blimey! How the hell am I ever going to get a guy to kiss my stretch marks if I can't get past first base by catching his eye? Okay, now I am back to thinking about my wobbly bits again!

I WILL NOT HAVE FLAPPY BITS CLAPPING WHEN I JUMP UP AND DOWN

Bit long winded that one. But the memory of that moment is forever etched in my (and Saskia's) memory. Urgh.

Thursday 28th May

I have to prepare myself for another big change. Am I ready? Hell no.

Saskia leaves tomorrow. She just got a new place to move to in London. It's the only way the kids can return home since our house is too small. I can't cope. I don't want her to leave, but I can't show her. She needs her space. It's what she wants and she also wants the kids to return back, as do I. It's been ten weeks.

I keep going upstairs to cry. I have to be strong. I don't want to eat, or drink, though I am eating more toffees than normal. The most beautiful thing was the walk we had this evening together. We laughed so much, but we are both so sad. We may never have this time together again…

Friday 29ᵗʰ May

I took S to London this afternoon. She had to move in before 4 p.m. to collect her keys. We got there at 3.55 p.m. Pushing the time as usual, but we kept finding an excuse to stay home longer. Neither of us was prepared for this moment. I had to be brave dropping her off and moving her in. I kept hugging her and telling her it was going to be great and a new adventure, reassuring and allaying her fears and concerns. Though I think those words were really spoken for me to hear. After all, she is moving during a time when our freedoms are limited.

As soon as it was time for me to leave, I couldn't let her go and kept finding an excuse to hug her. We both clung on far longer than we normally would. She was hiding her tears, whereas mine are impossible to conceal. I'm the most emotional person I know. I cry at *Moana* for goodness sake! She persuaded me to leave and I knew I had to, despite not wanting to go. So we hugged again and I got into the car for the journey home, both of us waving like mad at each other until I pulled out of view. Then I stopped the car, as soon as it was viable to do so and sobbed my heart out. I mean really wailed; the feelings of letting her go hurts so damn much. I loved our time together; it was a huge blessing and I want it back again, I don't want it to end.

When I got home, the house felt empty and cavernous, as though the heart had been scooped out of it. The feeling of lack and loss permeating the house was overwhelming. I went into her room and lay on the bed. I could smell her body spray and then I couldn't stop the tears from falling. I sobbed my damn heart out onto those pillows. I stayed there for at least an hour, lamenting the loss of her.

I called my psychologist friend Angus, who deals with loss at his clinic is Scotland. He held my hand through the feelings. He listened then imparted his wisdom; words I clung onto desperately for hope and guidance. I then drove to get myself some takeout food and a bottle of wine. I poured a large glass and flicked on the TV in the hope of finding something to distract my thoughts. However, focus wasn't coming and I kept flicking around the channels until I found something that appeased my monkey brain just enough to keep from jumping channels again. I run a bath, played some meditation music and tried to forget that for the first time in ten weeks, the house was deathly quiet at night.

<u>11 p.m.</u>
Diary I can't stop crying, it's awful. I miss her so much. For the first time in ten weeks of lockdown, I feel bereft and desperately lonely. Right now, I wish I had a partner, a support person in whose arms I could crumple into. Someone to hug me and tell me it's all going to be okay; that it's meant to be and that we are going to be fine; just fine.

Some days are great and other days like today, are shit. Life today feels like too much shit.

Saturday 30th May

I am walking around the house crying, no not just crying, but howling and sobbing. I'm a wreck, but I'm making myself useful. I'm sorting her clothes and air wrapping them into those air vac bags. She has so much stuff! I keep stopping to sob when I see the little knick-knack things she's kept from childhood. Every item takes me back to the days before her teenage rebellion kicked in. Before the bullying that changed her life forever. Before I started to lose my daughter to the grown up world neither she, nor I was ready for her to be in.

I call everyone I know, sobbing on the phone. Thank goodness for Angus, Rosa, David and Jenni. I couldn't face Andy, he wouldn't know how to respond. He'd probably tell me to go find a random guy and 'have a good shag.' That seems to be his antidote for every problem going. Not even a worldwide pandemic could stop his randy member from performing on a regular basis!

These guys have kept me going for the past two months. Rosa is the only one who lives anywhere near me, but she is isolating. Without them, my life would have been incredibly lonely and even more confusing. Before lockdown, I saw my London friends on a regular basis, but I no longer see them and the communication is almost irrelevant. Strangely, I am not missing that part of my life right now. I love the partying and networking, the dancing and going along to the big dress up events. But on a day-to-day basis, it is no longer as crucial to my life as I thought it was before. My kids, friends and my daily routines are the bread and butter on which I survive.

Despite my heart pain and the crushing sense of loss, I am so grateful for all the blessings I have received. The book about to be published, the time I have been blessed with to write and the space and freedom I have had for myself, which after eighteen years of being a mother, is incredibly rare. Those ten weeks with my oldest daughter were such a blessing and the knowledge that my other two were safe and enjoying time they didn't normally have with their father, was also a huge bonus. It meant I could concentrate on myself, and the pursuit of my own dreams, which I hadn't been able to do since having children. I was always just about coping; just barely surviving and always feeling like something was missing in my life. Perhaps that is to write? I don't know.

Despite my heart breaking, I do feel very grateful.

Sunday 31st May

This evening the kids returned home. I was worried they would struggle since my house is a fifth of the size of their dad's. But all is good. S is safe and says she is doing fine and already making friends in her house.

I do think my freedom just ended on some kind of level though. Tomorrow I take on the homeschooling mantle from my ex. Fair play to him for getting on with it, but alas it's now it's my turn. The ten-week holiday has definitely just come to an end!

It is so good to tuck my son up in bed though and give Lily enough hugs to cover two daughters. I really missed them.

Diary, I know it will all be okay. Just different from here on in, that's all.

Monday 1st June

I was awoken by Ben telling me his dream. Except it wasn't my normal 7 a.m. waking time, it was 3.25 a.m.! I listened patiently as I sat on the edge of his bed, then when he had finished expunging his dream memories, gently ordered him back to sleep. Ten minutes later, after a bathroom visit and snuggling back into bed to resume my sleep, he called out again.

'Mum...Mum...?'

'What Ben? Go back to sleep.'

'I can't sleep. I'm scared.'

I sigh. I am tired. My patience is being tested. 'Try.' I whisper loudly back.

Five minutes pass. I am waiting, my ears pricked in anticipation for the call. There is no call, only silence. I relax into my pillows and breathe out ready to attempt sleep again.

'I can't sleep. Can I come in with you?'

I lay there. It's something to four in the morning and I know within the next hour the sun will be slicing through the feebly constructed curtains and the dawn chorus will be pecking at my ears. I had to relent. The longer this went on, the more awake I was becoming.

'Okay, come on. But no snoring!'

Ben jumps into my bed, thanks and hugs me, he settled down into the pillow and breathes out in contentment. Within moments his breathing deepens and the room fills with the sounds of a 9-year-old's nasal packed snorts.

I pull the duvet over my head to drown out the sounds, only to be reduced to a sweaty mess. It was getting hot at night now early summer was hitting us hard. I tried to sleep. I over tried. I tossed one way, scrunched up another, lay on my back, my sides and then finally onto my tummy. This worked and I was soon asleep, until not long after, I was awoken again, this time by the duvet being yanked off me. I looked at Ben, who slept soundly and oblivious to the drama and sleep deprivation he was causing. I felt like crying. It was indeed, a rude introduction to no longer having the freedoms I had become acquainted to.

I was a tad bit grumpy when we finally woke up. I somehow slept through the dawn chorus but not the sun's sneaky striptease into the room. To be tired before starting a day that you know may already have the promise of being challenging, is not pleasurable. I was still emotional after the past few days and felt pretty exhausted. I so needed the good night's sleep I didn't just have.

And today Diary, I entered homeschooling hell...

Tuesday 2nd June

I haven't got a clue what I am doing with Ben's schoolwork. Seems Ben and his dad hadn't been doing the work online and instead, printing it all out and doing it on paper. I have all his work, but no one to give it to. The school wants it all to be submitted online.

Lily helped a bit, but confessed to not being involved in his work, since she was so focused on keeping up with her own. It's her GCSE year next term, so she has enough work to keep her busy.

81

I emailed the school for more information, passwords and just anything that could help us get started. In the meantime, whilst I was in full stress mum mode, Ben calmly turned on his Xbox and played Fortnite. Loudly! Thankfully, by mid afternoon, we were set up on his school site and attempting some of the work. It wasn't difficult, but it was time consuming and the English work required a lot of focus.

Diary, let me tell you about Ben. This boy is the most creative and 'out of the box' thinking child I have met. From as young as he could hold a screwdriver safely, he has been de-constructing and re-constructing things like toys, remote controls, cars etc. Sometimes they were brought back to life and other times they weren't. He could look at a cardboard box from the age of four and create something magical. At aged five he made and decorated a wearable Optimus Prime Transformer virtually by himself, out of one large cardboard box, a couple of smaller ones, some egg boxes, lots of foil and some paints. He's quite the creative soul. He also has the knack of being able to look at instructions and follow them without question, ever since he was very little.

He is so unlike me in that department. I once burst into tears and cried for half an hour solid, trying to construct an IKEA flat-pack unit. My daughter had to call one of my local friends to come help us, since I refused to come out of the bathroom until it was 'magically' constructed. That's how useful I am at instructions, DIY and techie stuff. I can change lightbulbs, it's just that I never do!

Often with creativity, comes lack of discipline in other areas, or simply perhaps, a disinterest. In Ben's situation, it's a total inability to sit still for more than five minutes before getting bored enough to jump from one chair to the other, or pretend to be a plane, a train or a superhero! Saskia thinks he has ADHD. I just think he has a creative soul.

Getting Ben to sit for two hours to do online schoolwork therefore, is like pulling teeth out with tweezers – long, slow and almost with no visible result! However, give him a creative task like drawing, making or constructing something and he can sit totally absorbed, for hours on end. And as for online computer games, getting him off his butt again and away from the screen, is a whole new matter.

So for the past two days, it has become quite the challenge this homeschooling lark. However, it's early days and I am sure we can master this. After all, he did it for ten weeks at his dad's. I am sure I can do this, no sweat. Right Diary?

<u>4.30 p.m.</u>
I just escaped upstairs to switch off my brain from the stress off schooling. I can now see why I did not become a teacher. I have no patience. Zero.

However, what I do have, is a very large brandy in my glass of diet coke. But nobody needs to know that right now Diary, just you and me. Wink wink. Cheers!

<u>11.45 p.m.</u>
I can just about see to write. I am beyond tired. I have been awake since forever. I am missing Saskia. I am missing the quiet. I am missing switching off my brain. I can see now that I would never have been able to write a book if Ben was here. I love him, I really do, but he is a full time occupation in himself.

Wednesday 3rd June

Before the kids woke up, I wrote a schooling timetable for Ben. Maths, English, break, Times Table Rock Stars, playtime and then spellings, lunchtime and then any afternoon school activity/lesson, followed by tech time or park time (his choice).

<u>11.25 a.m.</u>

The sun is scorching today. Lily got up, did an hour of work and then arranged to meet her friends in the park, for which she wants a lift at midday. Meanwhile, I am trying to get Ben to sit long enough to do his English. Lily stresses as she has left her summer shorts bag at her dad's and the only thing she wants to wear on her butt, is the cute denim shorts in that bag. Nothing else will suffice. Meanwhile, whilst she is stressing out and distracting me, I am being pulled away from Ben's work. He sees it as an opportunity to run and jump around and then get on his iPad and watch YouTube. I return to the table and nag Ben to return also. It takes forever and some tears. 'I hate doing English! I'm no good at English!' he yells loudly. Meanwhile, his sister walks into the living room, still stressed and moaning about not having anything to wear to the park.

I'm trying to stay calm, so take lots of deep 'I'm not getting stressed' breaths. I am also aware that the schedule, only up and running one morning so far, is already falling apart. In my head I am screaming 'Stick to the schedule, stick to the flipping schedule!' But the twisted knots in my tummy is screaming 'F the flipping schedule and go and eat some chocolate!'

Alas, the deep breaths didn't work. So instead, I scream at Ben, scream at Lily; tell them they will never amount to anything if they neglect their education, grab some chocolate from the cupboard and go outside and cry.

I am a total wuss and a failure at homeschooling and it's only been three days! I worked out that I have another seven weeks to go!

I called a teacher friend. She told me to do what I can with Ben then take him out when I dropped off Lily. 'You both need some fun', she declared. She was right.

'If you finish your English work, I'll take you to the skate park and get you some chips on the way home,' I told him.

It was a deal. I then left him to get on with it, since he had renewed enthusiasm suddenly. Not sure if it was the offer of taking his scooter to the park during school hours or the promise of chips afterwards, but he complied with my request and got on with it. Mental note – 'if all else fails, bribery works!'

Then I went upstairs to calm Lily down and help her find something to wear. Her dad was going to drop by later with the bag of shorts and summer tees. And once again, all was calm in the land of kids and mummy.

11.30 p.m.
Exhausted. Really wish I had a partner to share all this with me, but not sure I would have time for someone right now to be honest. One day please God? One day...?

Can't even look for or think about BOB!

Friday 5ᵗʰ June

Okay, had enough of playing teacher. Please can they go back to school? Pleeeeaaassee?

At least my book will be out on Amazon soon. Friend editing it for me, then I have to figure out how to publish it. Dreading that as much as I dread getting up to do school in the mornings. Weekend tomorrow. NO SCHOOL. Yay!!!!

Saturday 6ᵗʰ June

I survived a week of homeschooling. Oh boy. Seems my 9 year-old is the least focused, busiest and most distracted kid on the entire planet. Okay Diary, I exaggerate, but getting him to sit still for two minutes is hard enough, let alone two hours! Maths he can do (thank you God), since I am the least mathematically minded person I know other than his sister. Fancy that the only other person in the house to help with maths and tech, is neither mathematically nor technologically minded!

At least he's doing his times tables and his spellings. English I can do till the cows come home; it is my forte after all. Alas, it isn't his and everyday I feel I am digging for gold to encourage him to find the desire to do the work. I won't tell my ex this, but I really think I got the better deal not having the kids here for those first ten weeks; though only in terms of schoolwork of course. I missed the heck out of them every single day. But I really didn't miss the flipping schoolwork!!!

The weather though, is hot and blissfully sunny. Thankfully we aren't missing not having a holiday this year because we can go sit in the garden, or take to the woods for a picnic. Well I would if I could get my son out of the house! He misses his friends and since the only way he can connect with them is via online games like Fortnite and Minecraft, he is pretty obsessed with being in front of the box!

He keeps asking for a puppy. Maybe it's time to seriously consider getting one? I don't know though, it's such a huge commitment. And I'm already stressed to the hilt! Two kids home under confines of lockdown are bad enough. I would have to be mad to get a puppy, right??

Friday 12th June

Today I let Ben off homeschooling and instead we went to collect S from London. It's the first time I had driven on a long journey with him for three months. Crazy! We laughed and sang all the way there, as we sneakily borrowed his sister's beatbox (the kids laugh when I call her speaker that. Guess it definitely shows my age. Hah). That time with him in the car, was far more beneficial to his wellbeing than being stressed sitting in front of a computer to do work he really doesn't want to do.

I get it, I do, but boy do the kids need laughter and joy right now. It's the weirdest time in their lives and one day, in the not too distant future, I guess children will be reading about this in history books. The thought of it amazes my children. The idea that they are living through one of the most challenging, global humanitarian crises ever to hit mankind in present day history, is pretty surreal to them. And to me!

What I am really grateful for right now however, is the sunshine and hot weather. It changes everything and definitely makes lockdown living more bearable. We don't have much of a garden, more of a back and side yard really, but I am still so grateful to have this outdoor space. Lily sunbathes outside and then meets her friends to walk to the park or swim in the reservoir. Ben goes to the skate park most afternoons after his schoolwork, either with me or with his dad, who is able to juggle working from home with seeing his kids on a fairly regular basis.

Life is never easy or perfect. But I am grateful for it anyway. Gratitude has become a huge part of helping me cope with lockdown. I wish so much was different – that I had parents to care about and talk to (and also worry about, so at least I am spared that), a partner to share this with and to help support the children at home, a bigger home so we aren't all on top of each other and a job that brought in an income, or at least enabled me to qualify for those self employed government handouts.

BUT Diary...I am in such a better position than so many other people I know. And as my best mate always reminds me, I have my own teeth and hair! Mind you, with my new toffee addiction, I might be losing those teeth sometime soon and if I haven't pulled all my hair out at the end of all this, then I deem myself very lucky indeed.

<u>10.20 p.m.</u>
Left the girls to be girly and escaped upstairs. So hot today, so I am lying on my bed watching a chick flick in just my pants. There's a really handsome leading guy in this film. Oooh. I wish he was here right now, on this bed with me. What did that article from the beginning of lockdown say? *Sex with yourself is the safest sex.* Must remember that next time the house is empty!

Diary, when we come out of this, I am so joining a dating site again. I know I said I never would after the exasperation with all those bloody players and non-committal chancers I seem to meet, but it's been such a long time since I had a date. To sit in a restaurant or at a bar and actually have close conversation with a real person; get a kiss even. Oh I miss kissing and my sexual hormones are going crazy! Maybe I'm on the change?

Oh great. Horniness and menopause during lockdown... life just keeps getting better!

Monday 15th June

My book is officially on Amazon. Just want to leave that out there. I am AN AUTHOR!!! Whoopeeeee!

Saskia helped me get it uploaded yesterday, finishing close to midnight and although it was *slightly* stressful (seems I am very 'impatient' and 'stressy' – her words), we persevered and got it on.

One of my gin bottle donating admirers at the start of lockdown, pre-ordered a couple of signed copies and dropped round a bottle of champagne earlier this evening. Pink Bollinger – my favourite! Really made my day despite me having to reiterate that I am not an available option to him. You can't help whom you are and are *not* attracted too and he falls into the latter sadly. I opened it with him tonight though, since I really wanted a glass and wasn't going to drink it alone! I literally had to nag him to stay. I was that desperate for grown up company and it feels like it's been forever since I shared a drink with anyone. We socially distanced in the garden, which actually helped in terms of keeping any waylaid affection at bay. Thank you social distancing on this occasion!

Perhaps it's the champagne, but I feel flipping marvellous! I'm a published author! Finally, a dream I have had since I was a teenager, has actually just been realised. I just feel so elated right now. Nothing and no one is going to bring me down!

I AM AN AUTHOR!!!

Wednesday 17th June

Oh my! Bad hair day extreme!

Lily dyed my hair. I honestly thought I ordered the right stuff. I researched it and that's what Google told me to get. Can't get an appointment with a hairdresser for weeks after they open and my hair looks like I am growing snowdrops. So we decided to do a home dye job.

Thank goodness for Lily noticing that my roots were starting to get lighter not darker almost as soon as she had painted on the dye mixture. If she hadn't checked, my hair would have looked like a can of yellow paint had landed on it! We washed it out as quick as we could. All the while I was crying that I had ruined my hair and sobbing that not only did my boobs clap, but now my hair was going to look like a bleached washing up brush. Lily was trying not to laugh I could tell, but every now and then as I burst out sobbing with a 'Why me?' I could hear her snorting back her giggles.

We gave it three shampoos to be sure. Then I blow-dried it without looking. I was simply too scared. The idea of walking around for the next two months with bleached dyed roots over a brunette head of hair, filled me with complete dread. Hombre is one thing, sombre is another.

She caught it in time. It was lighter, but the dye/bleach mixture didn't have time to soak in to achieve a catastrophic (for me) result. Since I have a phobia about changing my hair style or colour anyway and only go four times a year to the hairdressers; two cuts and two root dyes, this was majorly stressful to say the least.

Diary, today was a bag of toffees and large glass of wine day. I'll be good tomorrow.

Saturday 20th June

I survived another week of homeschooling and increasing, crippling feelings of loneliness. Not even getting my book published can uplift me today. Lily went off with her friends early to the beach. Ben's dad collected him for a day out. It was just me and my face from 11.a.m. I went for a woods walk, but since I do that most days, it didn't feel so special. I tried to call my 'go to' friends, but only Andy picked up and all he had time to say was, 'Meeting Eliana and her friend today, so can we catch up tomorrow sometime?' That guy and his voracious penis!

Diary, I just have to do the gratitude list more often. I am so fortunate to have what I have, to live where I do and be safe and healthy. We are all lonely to some extent, even those rich and famous people who seem to have enviable lives. Perhaps part of the growth as a human being, is learning to see the sunshine despite the clouds?

For goodness sake, who have I become??

<u>Midnight</u>
How can I still manage to get tipsy, stay up late and still not be able to sleep, when I have no kids with me, which is the perfect opportunity to catch up on lost sleep? Apparently, lack of sleep is a lockdown norm. Will I ever be able to sleep a whole eight hours ever again?

On the plus side, I finally found BOB ☺

Monday 13th July

My books arrived! All seventy pre-ordered copies ready for signing this weekend. Can't wait for my friends to have my book in their hands. Everyone has been so supportive. I feel so blessed.

<u>10.45 p.m.</u>
Had a lovely evening.
Celebrated my books arriving, with a cheeky bottle of something with a friend on a bench in the woods this evening. I so loved getting a text from her saying that she wanted to personally collect her copy and that she was bringing a drink to celebrate. She'd really thought about it too – a decent pink Prosecco (my friends know me well) and disposable plastic cups. It was a beautiful, balmy summer's evening, with a background hum of wild bird chatter. Social interaction is so important for most species and something I have particularly missed. I'm a hugger, a snuggler, a hand

holder, a giggler and a lover of spending time with people. This lockdown period has been so challenging on so many levels. I am starting to see a light out of this tunnel. Just have to hold on a little bit longer.

So hot tonight, almost too hot for sleep; not that I sleep much anyway. Perhaps it's both the excited anticipation of an unknown future as an author, or simply the fear of the unknown, but tonight I feel so unsettled. Praying so hard right now.

Diary, how can I realise a childhood dream and yet also be feeling so uncertain about everything?

Thursday 16th July

Diary, today I went *out out*! My boss took a couple of us out for a meal in Soho. It wasn't the same crazy, busy hub of bustling tourist activity that I knew earlier this year, but it was so good to be away from Surrey and home and being a mum. Today wasn't about anyone else but me. Does that make me selfish, or simply a woman being herself without the labels of mother or slave to the home? If that does make me selfish, then please God, bring me more selfish days because I so loved being selfish today.

We had shellfish, oysters and Sancerre to drink to begin with. Well actually, the first thing I had, was a Cosmopolitan cocktail! Oh yes!!! The starter dishes were followed by a sea bass with Mediterranean style veg and samphire. Oh it was delicious. I even had a pudding - raspberry crème brûlée. Oh my, I felt so spoilt. And grown up! I miss this part of life so much.

I so love being in the production industry and it looks like there are some interesting projects coming up. Yes, can't wait. Finally, after months of lockdown and restrictions, hope is on the horizon!

Diary, I feel alive again. I have some hope. Or maybe it's just that my belly is full of fine wine, yummy cocktails and delicious food that wasn't cooked by me for a change?

Yes...hope. That lockdown is going to end soon. Hale-flipping-luia!

Friday 17th July

School is officially over. Thank flip for that, freedom at home finally. We celebrated with a trip to the beach this afternoon. It was so hot today. Ben hates the heat so the promise of cooler weather and a splash in the sea sent him into happy overdrive. Lily was just happy to get out into the sunshine and to have a drive somewhere.

I am ecstatically happy to see the end of home school. I definitely know now that becoming a teacher, was never my calling.

Celebrated with a gin o'cocktail this evening. It's Friday, it's the end of homeschooling, hopefully forever, and it seems I now really do like gin! That's definitely worth celebrating!

Tuesday 21st July

A day's production work in London. Yay! Grown up time. So exciting. Ex came to look after kids whilst I travelled by car, train and underground.

It's so quiet everywhere: eerie almost. The full on crazy hustling London I knew back in February, was so different to this ghost town of today. I didn't recognise the feeling of this place, despite having spent years travelling into this very station. The lack of social interaction and eye contact felt alien to me. Masks hid expressions and eyes were averted. I felt an irrational feeling of guilt, as though I were carrying the virus and was transmitting it to each passer by, simply by being there. I don't have it, am wearing a mask and adhering to all the rules, yet still I feel guilty. Not vulnerable, but instead, as though I were carrying around a secret. A bit like being the only one to know you aren't wearing any knickers! Oh boy, that takes me back. Fun memory that one! Couldn't do it now, not with my broken egg of a pelvic floor!

11.20 p.m.

It felt so good to work today. Oh boy, I so miss interacting with grown ups. I love my kids, but I also love my work persona. I like being the non-mum me. There may be more work next month and definitely in September. Perhaps things are finally starting to return to normal? I bloody hope so!

And my books are starting to sell slowly on Amazon, as well as friends and contacts still wanting to purchase signed copies. It's keeping my mind occupied if nothing else. I also love that some friends have left positive reviews on the book. Who knows, I might end up having a new career after all this is over? Not sure yet, but life is definitely more opportunistic than it was even before lockdown. How strange.

At least I haven't snacked once today and haven't even felt hungry. And the hot chocolate at the station whilst waiting for my train, meant I didn't pour a glass of something alcoholic tonight either. So working is good for me all round. And will certainly contribute to making me less 'round'! Damn my sweet tooth! And my crisp tooth and my wine tooth!

The kids are nagging for a dog. I'm starting to bend. Why I think we could fit a dog into our lives and into our bijou house, beats me? If I get a puppy Diary, I will be certifiably mad and have officially lost the plot.

Thursday 23rd July

We looked up puppies. The three breeds the kids chose are between two thousand and five thousand pounds. I am in debt, worked one day since beginning of March and can barely pay the rent. That put an end to that idea then. I think I am secretly relieved, though I didn't tell the kids since they were so disappointed.

Tonight Saskia came over and we made cocktails for old times sake. Oh my, have I missed those! Plus it's her birthday this weekend. That always requires celebrations. So we let the celebrations begin early. Well, *I* celebrated anyway, with three very generous cocktails and I don't feel guilty, just so darn happy for a change ☺.

Even S was trying to persuade me to get a puppy. What is wrong with these kids? Why do they always want more? I don't want a puppy in my already ridiculous life. I want work and a flipping man!

<u>11.50 a.m.</u>

Think I must be menopausal, or the one before that. What's it called? Peri peri pausal? Blimey, that doesn't sound right. Sounds more like a dish in Nandos. Ooh, I'd love to take the kids to Nandos. Please let us all go back to normality soon. And if anyone mentions 'the new normal' again, I'm going to bloody throttle them!

Okay, it's midnight again. I don't think I've managed to go to bed before midnight, EVER since lockdown started. So much for sticking to my resolutions.

<u>2.20 a.m.</u>
Must remember that adding diet coke to cocktails will result in hours of ceiling staring until you are forced to get up and drink copious amounts of water in order to flush the system. Too much alcohol and rubbish sleep – not a great combo for the next day. Mental note made and probably ignored the next time I am lucky enough to have cocktails!

Wednesday 29th July

Saskia's 19th and first lockdown birthday. Not much we can do, but thankfully we have the Eat Out to Help Out thing going so we booked a family meal at a local restaurant. Their dad came too (and generously paid). It was a lovely balmy summer's evening with lots of chatting and laughter.

No alcohol for me since I was driving. I've really slowed up on the drinking since Saskia left. I mainly over indulge on my weekends without the kids, since I am so flipping tired by the end of a day with them and a glass of anything leaves me dribbling and going 'bah bah bah' in my corner chair, staring like a mummified zombie at the TV. I've discovered what I already knew but always pretended I didn't, that there is rarely ever a break from being asked to do something, get something or look at something, as a mum.

Having birthdays with restrictions in place, hit home the weirdness of life in present day Britain. We have become so used to privileges like dining out, going to pubs and bars, being entertained at events, shows, cinema, festivals etc., meeting up with friends and family whenever we want (if you are fortunate to have that kind of family) and being able to jump in a car, on a train or plane, whenever we feel like it. My, how things have changed.

No matter how low I feel and I often do, I must always remember to reel myself back in with words and feelings of gratitude. Things could be so much worse and for many they are. The joy of social media, is that there is always a different perspective on offer to your own. The toughest part of course, is keeping an open enough mind to understand and appreciate that.

I have my own perspective on it Diary... If our situation were a circle and the virus a tiny dot in the middle, there would be many different segments of the circle all staring in at that central dot. I guess if it resembled anything, it would be like an orange, where each of the segments of the circle was a differing experience, opinion, perspective and viewpoint. And what if that circle was cut up so finely into even more differing segments, that instead of looking like an orange, it more resembled one of those delicious chocolate oranges, with much more segments than an normal orange? Ooh, I love chocolate oranges.

Reel it back Pen, stop thinking of your belly; focus...

Social media right now, feels a bit like that multi-segmented circle. The main issue with the social media 'orange', is that some of the segments believe they are more right and that all the other segments are wrong. And some segments seem to end up eating other segments and hence the circle becomes less like an orange and more like a circle graph. Suddenly, there is a majority segment and a few smaller segments filling up the circle shape. Who has the most power? Now, that is a very interesting question…

Diary, life is beyond weird right now and I don't want to live in an orange staring at a bloody virus that I wish someone would eat, shit out and flush down the toilet, so we can all get back to living our very misshaped and highly irregular lives.

Gosh my brain is an overthinking complex pile of mush and I don't think I will eat another chocolate orange ever again!

Monday 3rd August

Beautiful day, in so many ways; glorious sunshine, relaxed and chilled kids and not a bicker or gripe in sight. Ben went out with his dad and Lily met up with friends. That meant I had the whole day to myself. Bliss!

I went back to bed mid morning after they left and actually slept. The noisy neighbours and barking dog moved house on Saturday and so I was totally undisturbed for two hours of napping. I feel absolutely bloody amazing! It's divinely hot today with not a fluffy white cloud in sight. So I walked round the house naked. Yup. Completely starkers. AND IT FELT FABULOUS! Mind you, I refused to look in the huge mirror in my dining room for fear of ruining my happy mood. I swear I will NEVER jump up and down naked in front of a mirror ever again! I am still mortified that S caught me mid jump.

I will say though, that if one is going to walk around starkers in the house then one should definitely close the living room curtains before doing so. My 76-year- old neighbour who lives adjacent and shares a drive, which directly looks into our living room, nearly had a heart attack next to his new Land Rover Discovery. I swear he discovered a lot more about his single mum neighbour than he had bargained for that afternoon. Oh the shame!

Talking of discoveries, I must say, that Lily made an awesome one yesterday. If we position the sun lounger in a certain spot in the rear of our side garden, it is totally obscured from all prying eyes. That means that sunbathing 'au naturel' is a possibility. Since I always wanted to have a tanned bottom and not yet been in a situation to achieve that (until now), I was more than ready to take my chances today. No kids, hot sun, quiet neighbourhood, perfect environment for nude sunbathing.

Ah, hindsight is a wonderful thing.

Seems no one had told me that the back gate was used that morning to get a football from the garden for Ben's outing with his dad. And the door wasn't latched back up. In my defence for not checking, the gate is ALWAYS locked since I am a real stickler for security.

As I said, hindsight is a wonderful thing.

So there I am, stark naked on my lounger, in 28 degree heat. Water bottle at one side and a book I wasn't going to read on the other. I was lying on my front on a towel, a cushion propped under my lower tummy so that my bottom was slightly raised and had full exposure to the sun. I had oiled so I looked pretty juicy shall we say. Did I mention that the sun lounger directly faced the back gate, since that was the very spot that the sun hit without any preying eyes? And that my head faced the neighbour's adjoining fence, so that my backside was the one facing the gate? No? Ah, well...

I start to fall asleep. And why not, I was unusually alone and these moments are rare and ripe for taking advantage of. I felt a draft. Strange I thought, since there wasn't a cloud in the sky and no wind. I ignored it, since it actually felt quite lovely. I opened my legs a little to let in some of that welcome breeze. Yes, that felt much better. It was getting a little hot down there anyway.

I could feel myself starting to drift off, but was startled suddenly by a noise coming from the drive. It felt very loud and close. My initial thought was that it was fine, since I was completely hidden by the gate, but then a sick feeling arose in my gut. That breeze...

I turned my head and was horrified to find the gate had subtly blown open to reveal my nether regions directly onto the street. And the noise on the drive was the postman about to deliver his post – to my house.

Well...you have never seen a forty-seven year old woman move as quickly as I did! I swear in a blink of an eye, I was up off that lounger and hiding round the corner, still completely starkers, but at least concealed from the postman's view. Despite being able to be seen by at least five different

101

neighbour's windows (if they looked), I darted butt naked inside the house and upstairs quicker than you could say 'Holy bollocolies!'

I don't think he saw me, but this is the 25 year-old postie who already had an older woman crush on me before this.

Diary one day I will laugh about this, but for now, you are the only one I am ever telling this to, so this is mega secret! Wait...I am telling my diary this and making it swear never to tell anyone else???

Oh boy...I really am Shirley Valentine in more ways than one. That, or I have completely lost the plot!

Thursday 13th August

Not much to write about Diary since the days are so similar. No school, hardly any work and little money to do anything if there was anything to do anyway. Most afternoons I take Ben to the park and Lily is always with her friends. Saskia is having as much of a great time in London as she can, given the restrictions, but teenagers find their way. They are far more resilient than we give them credit for.

I do the food shopping and rarely take the kids with me. The kids eat and eat and snack like their lives depend on it. So I am at the shops most days. Who'd have thought that going to the supermarket would be the new *out out?*

We did have a laugh earlier though. Okay, the kids laughed at my expense. They tried to teach me to twerk! Now bearing in mind, that I have a stiff back from an old sports injury from my twenties, and I am more tum than bum, so then, twerking is not the easiest dance move for me to master. Even Ben does the twerk better than I can.

Not wanting to be a spoilsport, I tried it. On went the music, up lifted my top, which was duly tucked into my bra, so that I could see what my bum was meant to be doing. The music played and off this mum went. Well, it was nothing short of a disaster. I nearly fell over the dining room chair that I was holding onto, wet my overly tight lycra shorts from peeing with the sheer effort of trying to make my bottom jiggle and almost put my back out trying not to follow the falling chair onto the ground. Seems the chair wasn't sturdy enough to withhold this woman's body pounding awkwardly against it. The kids were rolling around in hysterics, which then set me off laughing so hard I properly peed myself. Oh the shame of being me. Stiff limbed and lose pelvic floored. Total mess.

Please God may I find a guy before my pelvic floor sinks below ground level and my pants are full of urine soaked mama pads. Oh and before the menopause too, since I am peri peri that one already.

Friday 21st August

Last night I made the decision to take all three kids away for the weekend. The weather is glorious and I wanted to give them some kind of holiday this summer since we cannot go abroad. Besides, my book is selling fairly well for an unknown author and had my first sales commission paid in a couple of days ago. Not huge, but enough to treat us to a couple of days away and a night in a hotel in our favourite part of Dorset.

I got up early and we left later than planned. That's what happens when you have teens in the house. Getting up early for them, is 11 a.m. Whereas Ben is up with the larks and the cooing pigeons (on the roof opposite my bedroom window – I swear I could shoot them sometimes!).

The best part of going away in this country with my kids, is the outward car journey. The warmth of expectation permeates each child and within minutes of starting off, music is blasting through Lily's Bluetooth speaker and we are all bouncing around inside the car. I can only move my shoulders, head and left hand, but I've pretty much nailed my moves!

These are the best of times. I love feeling the sense of excitement oozing from the children. There is always a snack bag and the sweets, crisps and chocolates are soon being passed around. Laughter and tunes ring out from our old, battered Saab, with wind down windows and air con that gave up the ghost at least two summers ago. It was hot; so hot in that car, but we didn't care. We were going on a little holiday; a break from the house and a feeling of life returning us back to normal.

We drove straight to the beach. Along with EVERYONE ELSE in England it seemed. Blimey! It took us an hour and a half to get through the beach road and then find somewhere to park. The pleasure of that privilege alone was £12. There was only one toilet and one shop at this part of the beach and no cashpoint, since I had completely forgotten to take out any money before we left. Going to the cashpoint is a rarity these days as using cash is almost as frowned upon as hugging. Thankfully we didn't need cash, since the shop and the ice cream van were not taking cash payments!

Such a gorgeous day, in so many ways. This part of Dorset has a huge, long beach, so we didn't feel cramped. The kids had fun and I think I read one page of a book since Ben was in and out of the sea all day as per the norm. The girls loved their time together and watching them all forget the global situation for just a few hours, made my motherly heart swell. For the first time in a while, I felt like it was all going to be okay.

Then the evening came. What a shame things got ruined. I'm a last minute, spur of the moment woman. Usually that works fine for me, but not in a global pandemic, where there are restrictions on where to eat and your daughter happens to be a coeliac, so then, finding somewhere serving gluten free food, becomes a target objective.

The cute pub bed and breakfast I booked did not cater for gluten free. I did check that they did, but I saw the online menu and failed to call up to check. They were only offering a reduced menu and it did not cater for allergies ☹. That's okay Diary, I am nothing if not resourceful. So we got dressed up and headed out. Three kids and myself would normally cost a bit to eat out, but with the Eat Out to Help Out on, it would be fine. Except this was 7 p.m. on a Friday and it wasn't a qualifying day. 'That's okay' I told them, 'needs must, I'll treat you'. Except that I hadn't accommodated for the whole of England also deciding to visit that area and with the new restrictions in place, we couldn't find a restaurant with an empty table for miles.

The kids were starving by now, having only snacked all day. Tempers were starting to flare and the bickering levels were ascending. It was getting ugly in the Wood family. They needed distraction. I had a brainwave.

'Let's drive around and find a place.' So we did. For over an hour. By 8.15 p.m., nobody could look at each other and the only radio station we could get working, was pretty dire, even for my eclectic taste in music. My tummy was growling and my head pounding from the bickering and the stress. I was at a loss of how to feed these kids. Finally Saskia came up with a plan.

'Let's get Ben kebab and chips and us three can have a chicken korma. It's gluten free.'

'Yes!' they all screamed in union. So I guess that was the plan then.

By the time we got our orders and sneaked them up to our big family room, it was just past 9 p.m. The whole episode of hunting for food, took two hours and a lot of miles of driving. The irony in all this though - we went through a main city, three towns and a couple of villages, before finally arriving back in the village we were staying at, where side by side, stood a kebab shop and a curry house. I kid you not, a fifteen-minute walk from our B&B accommodation. You couldn't write this stuff Diary. Hah. I just did. Now that's ironic!

11 p.m.

I am snuggled in bed next to Ben listening to his gentle snores. He smells of the sea, since he was too tired to bathe when we got home. The girls and I showered when we got back from the beach before heading out. I could hear the girls giggling in the other room from their single beds. Outside, the rushing cars on the cut through road beside the pub, had slowed to just the odd vroom. All was quiet in the land of the Woods.

This parenting lark is probably the hardest, most exhausting and emotionally demanding job I have ever had, but without doubt, also the most gratifying. I am so grateful for my children and my blessings God, thank you.

Okay Diary, these woman's lights need to go out early tonight. Another long day ahead tomorrow, navigating the highs and lows of single parenting, on a weekend away during a flipping global pandemic.

Monday 24th August

The kids spent the weekend nagging me to get a dog. I tried to explain that since it is just me in the house when they return to school (please God that they return) and that I am a freelance worker relying on flexibility at home to be able to work, that it wasn't really possible for me to also be a fur mummy.

They kept on. I think kids have tunnels especially built inside their ears to allow the words of parents, to filter straight out without stopping. The tunnels were in full force today, since none of my pleas against the argument were sticking.

I heard all their pro-arguments for getting a puppy, yet they didn't hear my one against – my precious time!

I told a couple of friends. One said 'don't', the other said 'do'. I told them both the price of puppies these days due to the lockdown situation and they both said a resounding 'don't!'

So that's it; mind made up. We are definitely not getting a puppy!

Wednesday 26th August

Someone up there is having a laugh with me. The friend who at first said yes to me getting a dog, then no when she heard the prices, called me today. Her friend's friend is a Labrador breeder and lo and behold, she has a spare puppy. The bitch (not the friend) gave birth to an extra unaccounted for pup. So, if I want one for a normal price, all I have to do is message the breeder. I told the kids' dad who agreed to go halves. I had just sold two paintings so I have a deposit sitting in my account. Is this providence?

Oh the dilemma!!!

Diary, what do I do? On one hand, it would be so good for the kids to have the distraction of a puppy. Lily is down about returning to school under the restrictions, Ben is nervous about starting in his new school and not knowing anyone and Saskia has her own life in London but has always wanted a dog, so she says it will encourage her to come back more. On the other hand, there are all the reasons why I don't want another mouth to feed or another body to think about. Is that selfish of me? Do I have the right to put myself first before them? Argh. Why aren't there fairy godmothers to help out with these kinds of things? After they've done the dishes, swept the floors and cleaned the bathroom of course. Really must pray for a fairy godmother, after all, there's not much difference between Cinderella and myself at the moment. Except I can't sing!

Thursday 27th August

Still haven't decided. Slept so badly last night, which is pretty much the norm most nights anyway, but particularly rubbish last night. I haven't told the kids. I can't bring myself to get their hopes up if I then change my mind. I have to let the breeder know by tomorrow afternoon the latest as she has a waiting list. I jumped the queue because it was a friend of a friend of a friend!

I've been so good lately, but today is an alcohol day. No doubt about it. I need all the help I can get for this decision.

<u>Midnight</u>

I'm wavering to the kids' side. I've called or messaged everyone whose opinions I respect. Although I did call Andy and that was a whole other conversation.

Andy – 'You might meet someone dog walking Pen. Think about it.'

Me – 'Mmm. It's such a risk though Andy. What if I get loads of work and then am committed to the dog and can't commit to the job? What do I do then? I've already lost so much work and I'm already waist high in debt.'

Andy – 'Live on the wild side girl. Take risks. That's what life is all about! When was the last time you took a big risk honey and it paid off?'

Me – I was thinking for quite a while. 'Er...well, I'm not really a risk taker Andy, you know that, but there was one risk I took a couple of years back. I don't think I've told you.'

Andy – 'Oooh you devil. Go on, tell me, I'm all ears. Did it pay off for you?'

Me – 'Er, no…not exactly. No.'

Andy – 'No? So what was it? What happened? Come on, spill your guts…' he has such a way with words.

Me – 'It involved a guy.' I could hear Andy squirm with delight down the other end of the line. 'It was August 2018. I had met this guy through a mutual friend on social media. We got messaging and soon found we had a lot in common. He lived up north somewhere and worked as TV producer.'

Andy – 'He sounds perfect. What happened?'

Me – 'On paper he was. That's the thing. We shared the same taste in music, things we watched, work, humour…'

Andy – 'Crucial. He has to make you laugh Pen,' he added, 'no point if he doesn't have humour.'

Me – I laughed. 'Indeed! But, he wasn't who he made himself out to be.'

Andy – 'What happened? Did you meet up? Come on girl, tell me!'

Me – 'So, as you know, I was really struggling financially back in 2018. I had spent all my savings on re-training for my costume work and was earning a pittance as a production runner. I think most of what I earned went on travel and childcare. My ex had taken the kids away to Greece on holiday and I was at home, since I couldn't afford to go away by myself. So when this guy called and asked me to visit for a couple of days, I didn't think twice and just said yes.'

Andy – 'Penelope Wood! You wanton hussy you! Go on! And there's me thinking you were a little prude.'

Me – 'I'm only a prude with you Andy, because you are such a tart who constantly tries to shock me!'

Andy – 'I don't have to try darling. You are mortified at most of the things I get up to!' He wasn't fibbing, he really did continue to surprise me. 'So, you went up and what happened.'

Me – 'So it's *how* I went up. I took a bus; the cheapest possible return ticket I could find. It was a late night bus to this guy's city, and we are talking very late. He had to collect me from the station in the early hours of the morning. It was a very long journey as he lived in Newcastle. I hadn't slept a wink either, as the seat I had been allocated was next to the window and there was a horizontal bar on it, so I couldn't lean up against it comfortably. Plus I left my coat in the roof rack above my head so couldn't use that as a substitute pillow. And the reason I couldn't get up to get my coat, was that the man next to me, who wouldn't stop talking for the first hour, had fallen asleep and his heavy bag had pinned my left leg down so I couldn't move. I would have had to wake him and risk him talking to me again. And his breath smelt of poo. Literally.'

Andy – 'Oh Pen. Sounds horrendous. How much was the ticket?'

Me – '£33 return.'

Andy – 'Well girl, you get what you pay for!'

Me – 'Shut up Andy. It was a nightmare. My head kept banging against the window, my left leg had horrendous cramp and the guy just behind me was snoring as though he had a trumpet stuck up his nose! Plus someone kept farting in their sleep and it stank! Never again! I swear, I will NEVER do one of those flipping cheap bus trips ever again!'

Andy – Sounds of giggling. 'Sorry Pen. Continue with the story.' Chuckles even louder, but this time with a snort. 'So you finally get off the bus and there waiting for you, is Mr Charming TV Producer looking all fresh and ready to whisk you off for a romantic weekend. Am I right?'

Me – 'No. Well, yes, he was waiting, but no he was not the Mr Charming TV Producer he made himself out to be.' Andy is trying hard to conceal his giggles but isn't doing such a great job. 'Shall I continue. It does get worse?' I ask impatiently. Why did I start telling him this story anyway?

Andy – 'It gets worse?' Now he is cracking up. I really could punch Andy right now. I'll save it for when I next see him. In fact, I owe him a few and it'll be good to release some pent up energy on a tart like him. I'll do it in the name of feminism and womankind.

Me – 'Thing is, I had spoken to him on numerous occasions, seen photos of him and of course, studied his social media profiles. But when I met him, he was nothing like the person I imagined him to be.'

Andy – 'How come?'

Me – 'Well, he told me he was 5 foot 11 and slim. And all his photos showed a dark haired, beardy man.' Andy by now is cracking up, since he has guessed what's coming next.

Andy – In-between splutters of laughter he asks, 'And who exactly did *you* get?'

Me – 'Not that person!!!' Andy can't help himself by now and I also break down into a laughing fit. In-between tears of mirth, I explain how the person who stood before me, was no bigger than me (5 foot 3), had what one could now describe as 'a lockdown belly' ripening over his overly-taut denim jeans, a very balding salt and pepper head and a clean shaven face to reveal the widest Desperate Dan chin I had ever seen close up! He was a little smelly, which he blamed on a curry and beers with his mates the night before. In fact, he mentioned that he had only had a couple of hours sleep since he was at a mate's party and was having too great a time to leave. I think I was too shocked to care. Only one thought was going through my mind – that I still had thirty-six hours with this man before I could get back on a bus home again.

Andy – 'Oh pen. I haven't laughed so much in ages. You really do crack me up! What did you do? Did you manage to get back on a bus or train? You weren't going to stay there were you?' Silence. 'Noooo! Say you didn't stay?' Silence. 'Oh Penelope Wood, you are so going to have to write a story about your life one day. You make me die!'

Me – 'Well what else could I do? I had to stay. I had £20 in my purse as he said he would look after me when I was up there.'

Andy – 'And did he?' he asked between fits of laughter, adding, 'OMG my cheeks are killing me from laughing so hard.'

Me – 'No of course he didn't. He had less money than me.' By now, even I was in fits of giggles. Tears were rolling down my face, since we couldn't stop laughing. It was hysterical. Only Andy can make me laugh this hard. He's worth keeping around just for moments like this.

I told Andy how the guy was actually not a TV Producer, but an extra and a production grip's assistant. Apparently he always wanted to be a producer, so decided to tell everyone he was, so that his wish could come true. I see where his mind was with that, but the reality was much different. He made these little personal films about his days, which were bloody awful and so boring that I fell asleep watching one of them! His flat was ridiculously teeny and I ended up sleeping on a couch that was barely big enough for two bums let along my stretched out body. There was no way I was sharing a bed with him. The most awful part of the weekend, was having to be upfront and tell him that I didn't fancy him, but since I was there, we should enjoy the time anyway. I hoped we could be friends, at least until I got back on the bus.

Alas, it wasn't what he wanted to hear. So he didn't feed me or take me out as planned. The area he lived in was a miserable, run down place on the edge of the city. I tried going out for a walk, but I felt safer inside with Mr Not Who He Said He Was.

Me – 'I swear, I will never do anything that stupid again Andy. So as for getting a dog...I just don't know. It seems less of a risk than jumping on a bus to meet some weirdo in a different part of the country.'

I left Andy howling with laughter. I had to go. The kids were coming home from a day out with their dad to get school shoes.

<u>9.45 p.m.</u>

I think I need to spend time praying and meditating. Amazing how relaxed one can be with a large glass of wine whilst meditating ;-)

Friday 28th August

Last night I had a dream. I saw two big hands deliver a golden Labrador puppy to me and behind the puppy, were two huge silver wings.
My mind was made up. I emailed back and said yes to the puppy. Then I went to tell the kids.

<u>10.40 p.m.</u>

I am the most popular mum on the planet right now. I still think I am mad though. Blimey Diary. What have I done? Too late to turn back now…

Tuesday 1st September

Kids go back to school tomorrow Diary. I am a sorrowful mixture of relief, excitement and sadness. How can I be sad when I have had kids at home with me since mid March? Honestly, I confuse myself sometimes. Here I am crying because I am going to miss the very kids I could have throttled yesterday for bickering and winding each other up all day.

Being a woman and being a mother are the most complicated things to be right now I have decided. At least I have a few days work booked in for this month and I am thinking about starting an online screenwriting course. One thing this pandemic has taught me, is that I need to have a few options available if we are ever thrown into situations like this again. I can write from home if I can't go to work, so it makes perfect sense to re-train to have a career where I am my own boss and can work from my own sofa. It's an idea anyway.

Diary, I am going to go cuddle my babies downstairs and pretend that I haven't been crying ☹

Wednesday 2nd September

Dropped the kids to their schools. It felt so weird today coming home to an empty house. I made myself a cuppa and sat down and listened to the silence. Instead of it feeling like bliss, the silence was howling through the house like the groaning sound of wind whirling through a cave.

I drank my tea and took myself for a walk into the woods. I called Rosa and sobbed. She was working from home, but her meeting had just ended so could listen. I love Rosa. I thank God every day for Rosa and her decision to pick up my call whenever she is able. She bestows such amazing wisdom and advice on me and has definitely kept me on the straight and narrow, and sane (though that is debtatable). I know I wouldn't have made half the crazy mistakes I've made if I had her in my life earlier.

I called David too. His advise - I had to get back on my train. Mustn't get off. He reassured me that the kids going back to school, is a good thing and nothing to be sad about. They need it and I need it.

Okay Diary, I am going to utilise this time by myself before the puppy comes and whilst work is picking back up, and get myself stuck into learning. Time to find me that screenwriting course!

Thursday 3rd September

Kids already doing my head in. So glad they are back at school. Can't believe I was sobbing yesterday. I'm such a wuss. Must get a grip on my life. Seize the day Pen. And seize the flipping freedom!

Tuesday 8th September

There's a new DPD delivery driver on our route. Oh my Diary, he's lush. And with the rate that Lily keeps ordering things online from Amazon and accounting for a fraction of Bezos' newly found pandemic fortune, I might be seeing a lot more of him. I wonder what I need online? The girls have been nagging me to update my wardrobe for ages, so I could splash out and treat myself maybe? They are nagging a lot lately and I'm not great at batting off their pleas, as the soon-to-be new fur addition to the family proves.

Time to make some new resolutions:

I AM A STRONG MOTHER
I AM THE BOSS OF THE HOUSE
WHAT I SAY GOES AND NOT WHAT THE KIDS SAY
I WILL NOT BE NAGGED INTO SUBMISSION
I AM GOING TO START ORDERING ONLINE

Mmm. Where did that last one come from?

Saturday 12th September

Kids at their dad's this weekend. I have nothing planned. Can't really go anywhere and most of my close local friends are still shielding. Waiting for an order of my books to arrive so I can go on a few book-signing events at the end of this month and next. So excited about that. Plus I start the screenwriting course later this month and I have five more days' production work ahead. Life is good if I compare where I am now to where I was just a month ago, so how come I still feel without purpose and lonely?

Maybe I should join a dating site? Tonight I will take a look when I've had a couple of glasses of wine. I am now only allowing myself to drink on weekends. Though truthfully, I have broken this on many an evening! Must work harder at sticking to my own rules! Oh and better start wearing a bra. I have noticed that my boobs have definitely edged closer to my belly when I am sitting down. Should also start brushing my hair more often too and maybe book a haircut, since I haven't had one since last November. Oh dear, I've actually become a slob!

Monday 14th September

My books arrived today, just as the government's 'Rule of Six' began. Flipping great! Now I have to cancel my planned book signing events and I have a hundred books to sell and nowhere to sell them. And there's also the credit card bill to pay at the end of the month for the purchase of the books.

Argh! Bugger, shit and fanny flaps! Right Coronavirus, you can go do one now. I'm officially over this flipping virus thing!

Must remember Diary that the government knows what they are doing right? Though Andy did make me laugh earlier when I spoke to him about the books and the Rule of Six.

Andy – 'I wish Spitting Image was back on.'

Me – 'Why's that?'

Andy – 'Well, with our 'interesting' PM and ministers with names like Hancock and Cummings and a stone faced guy called Whitty, there's enough material there to keep them going for months.'

Me – 'Hah, yes! True. Oh my, I never made the correlation with any of those names. How funny. I'm surprised nobody has taken the mickey yet.'

Andy – 'Pen really? Where have you been? Haven't you seen the memes?'

Me – 'Er...no. I don't really watch much telly.' I was guessing it was some type of satirical programme or sitcom on TV.

Andy – Laughing (he always laughs in our conversations. I'm sure I'm not *that* funny?) 'Oh Lordy hun. sometimes, I swear you live under a rock where these little sweet fairies are making you fairy tea and tying daisies together to make chains to go around your neck.' He continues to laugh.

Me – 'Ah, that sounds sooo good!'

Andy – Sighs in exasperation. 'Gotta go take a call from the U.S. Big producer wants to collab. Great times ahead Pen. Don't give up and remember there are many ways to skin a cat!'

Well what does that mean? Why would I even want to skin a cat? What was the man on? I thought we were talking about funny names of ministers and not being able to sell my books? Why am I suddenly going to skin a cat? Honestly, I think the guy has a screw lose somewhere in that single-minded head of his!

Gosh, I wonder if they really will be re-making Spitting Image? And I must pay more attention to politics and maybe watch the news every now and then. I haven't a clue who any of these people are. Maybe Andy was making up the names? Though I had heard of Cummings because of a hoo-ha about a Castle trip somewhere up north. I don't know, it's all gobbledegook to me. But perhaps I really should make more of an effort to know what's going on in government? New resolutions to add to the continually growing list that I forget to look at:

I WILL BE MORE POLITICALLY AWARE

I WILL BE LESS POLITICALLY IGNORANT

I MUST LOOK AT MY RESOLUTIONS LIST AT LEAST ONCE A WEEK

There you go! A new, more aware and less ignorant me to look forward to!

Thursday 22nd September

Perhaps it's providence or maybe coincidence, since yesterday I was talking to Jenni and she said she had started dating a guy she met on a dating site. I hadn't heard from her in ages though I had sent messages, but she is often elusive so I left her be. Seems she was busy with her messages from potential dates. Good for her. Life is short and nothing is guaranteed, as we have already witnessed this crazy year.

Anyway, back to providence... I received an offer for a free month sign up for a dating site. Well, I couldn't turn down a free offer! So I signed up and tonight I received messages from seven guys. Wow! Two were under the age of 30, so they were immediately discounted. One I had seen doing the rounds on the varying sites for the past 2 years (which also means I have been doing the same, though truthfully, more as an observer than a participant), so he was definitely discounted. Who needs a serial player with commitment issues? Been there and never going there again. Another of the potential dates didn't look like someone I wanted to spend a moment with let alone an evening out; a shame, since on paper, he had many of the qualities I was looking for. That left three guys who had real potential. I messaged them all back and so we will see who responds and where it goes.

I am not holding my breath. I have been here too many times before and every single time, I leave the site wishing I hadn't wasted my precious hours in streams of going nowhere conversations.

Nobody can say I am not trying. Maybe I should just accept that I could end up being single for the rest of my life? Is that so bad?

Arghhhhh!!!

Time to dream of Brad I think. I could just tell him I'll keep my own surname? That might work!

Friday 23rd September

We've been having such a lot of parcels delivered this week. Gotta love my daughter's new addiction. And now mine! What a shame I had to see the new DPD driver three times in the past few days. Hehe. Still it did get us chatting a bit. Got his name (Matt) and some info about him. Turns out he's actually an actor and mature model (explains the good bone structure) and is doing the delivery driving until the industry work picks up again. Let's hope it doesn't pick up before we exchange numbers hey Diary? ;-)

How lovely to finally meet a guy whom I have something in common with. Well, a lot in common actually. Okay, I know it's only been brief chats since he has to rush off to do his deliveries, but I can tell he's interested too. Oh how exciting! Can't wait until that new book I ordered arrives on Monday. Hehe.

Diary, I am getting into a new routine of going to the coffee shop, writing and reading. Life is nowhere near normal, but with this gorgeous Indian Summer weather, the kids at school and a bit of work to keep the cupboards stocked up, the mental bruises from the last six months are starting to heal. Lockdown is properly over. Restrictions remain and the social distancing and masks are still in place, but on the whole, life *feels* better.

Bought myself a book on how to teach myself screenwriting before the course starts next week. I sold another small painting, which paid for the course. And the three things from Amazon I ordered are arriving on Monday! Wink, wink.

Yup, life is back on the up. Thank fraggle rock for that. Might celebrate with a cheeky bottle of fruit cider tonight. I've been so good with not drinking in the week and reduced it hugely on the weekend. I'm almost back to my pre-lockdown days. And I've not eaten a toffee for almost 2 weeks! Okay, I know it's because my tooth started to hurt, but at least I stopped! I was worried I was developing an addictive nature.

<u>1.15 a.m.</u>
I am beginning to wonder however, if I am addicted to trawling through the dating site on the hunt for THE ONE! It's gone 1 a.m. and I've only just come off. I've been on since 10.45 p.m.

I do quite enjoy the banter with one guy called James. He's really has caught my attention...

Saturday 24th September

The weather is amazing! Lily went to the beach with her friends and Ben and I mooched. We watched a film on Netlfix and then headed off to the park with his skateboard. He met his mate and I was able to fall asleep in the car park for an hour, with the sun warming my face. Oh much bliss is that?

I'm relaxing a lot. Not writing, earning some money and having more free time to myself, means I am doing things I wasn't justifying doing before – watching Netflix and sleeping in the day for example (I have a LOT of sleep to catch up on). Last year I was constantly in London, either working or networking for work: so much rushing around to squeeze as much as I could into my days. Now I feel as if I am floating through life. I've become a bit of a Netflix series addict (oh boy, there's that word again…). So far, I've watched *Grace and Frankie* with S who loves it, *Dead to Me* and *You* with Lily who told me about the latter and really shouldn't be watching it! I've also been recommended *Afterlife* by Ricky Gervais. That's next on my list.

I don't do this Diary. This relaxed, chilled out person isn't me. I'm the stressed, chasing my tail, always pushing myself to the limit woman who never seems to stop, eat properly or sleep. Apart from the sleeping bit, which is still completely erratic, I now do all those things I didn't do before and some to excess, like eating way more in one week, than I used to do in three! No wonder all my bits are still bouncing in front of the mirror. I know I said I wouldn't do it again Diary, EVER, after that time S saw me, but it's become a bit of a habit every time I pass my bedroom mirror naked. A gross addiction of mine that I really must stop! Damn…that addiction word again. I think I'm getting paranoid. It's definitely my overthinking going overboard through the boredom and restrictions.

I wonder if there is an equivalent of the addiction rooms for toffee eating and jumping up and down in front of a mirror naked watching your boobs clapping? If there is, wonder if you have to wear a mask and social distance? In fact, how are people getting together for groups like that, if even churches and religious places are closed for gatherings and worship? Is everything now online? Can you imagine if dating itself became an online only thing? How do you share a kiss online? Wonder if that will actually become a thing?

Time to sleep. My head is off doing obstacle runs again. It's definitely time to switch off the overworking brain!

No messages on the site tonight. Wonder where all the guys are?

Thursday 1st October

October already. Wowzers! Ben turns 10 this month and we get a puppy in 2 weeks and I am pretending to myself that I'm not completely anxious about it. I am making the most of these lazy days until then. Just started the screenwriting course this week and already I am loving it, since it's so interesting. I can really feel like my life is taking on a new path with this. Who knows Diary, perhaps I'll be writing a screenplay on being a lockdown mum one day? After the past 6/7 months, I'd pretty much say that nothing could be ruled out and that everything is possible!

Tuesday 6th October

Matt the delivery guy and I had a good old natter today. I told him what I do as a career and I couldn't stop him talking! Seems he doesn't meet many people in our field of work living in this area. Tell me about it!

I like that he's chatty. And he's funny. Trying not to like too much about him though, as I still don't know if he's single or not. Men can be so sneaky, as I found out with Richard. I hope I never see that man again, but I must confess that I haven't entirely got him out of my head. Still working on that.

Until I do find out more about him, I've decided to play it cool. I almost wrote 'easy' but I really don't think being easy is the way to go if I want to meet a decent guy who is looking for more than a quick hook up! Yup, nonchalant and laid back is the way to go with Mr DPD Man. Though he did say he liked cakes...maybe I should make him some of my famous rock cakes?

Reel it in Pen, reel it in.

<u>11.45 p.m.</u>
Watched a film with Lily who should have been revising for her mocks at the end of November. But she needed some mummy time. We grabbed loads of snacks, made tea and snuggled in her duvet. These are the best of times.
Then I had a bath and a cheeky glass of wine. Yes I know it's Tuesday, but tonight I needed something. I feel a bit edgy. Perhaps my period is due?

Wednesday 7th October

I have been asked on a date! James from the site asked me. So exciting! We booked it for next weekend, since I am only able to meet up when I don't have the kids. He lives in Essex, so we decided that London was a great place to meet up for a drink. Yes, a date and in London! Oh I can feel normality seeping back into my veins. Thank flipping goodness for that!

Wednesday 14ᵗʰ October

London is going into Tier 3 tomorrow and that means the planned production work has been postponed. There goes my work for the foreseeable future.

Bugger, shit and fannyflaps! Argh.

That money was so needed – for the puppy purchase and all the paraphernalia that goes towards the expense of having one, for Ben's birthday later this month, for paying the credit card for the purchase of my books. And I can't even think about Christmas!

The books are selling slowly, but it's going to take a while to make back the money I spent. Fancy becoming an author during lockdown! If these were normal times, I'd be touring the country doing book signings and organising book events. Oh well. These are definitely NOT normal times.

Diary, this situation isn't new to me so I know I have the tools to cope. I've lost income twice before and so I can do this can't I? I'm strong and resilient and I know I can get through these times. BUT... sometimes I just want to get off this mummy hamster wheel and sit in the corner of the cage with a hamster margarita, a sun lounger (with the sun beating down on me) and a good book. Okay now I have an image of hamster me reading. Not such a great analogy comparing myself to a rotund, cocktail drinking, book reading hamster. Must work on getting my brain back to a more sensible place. It's gone a bit haywire lately!

Oh the thought of a holiday though: to escape to a wee little island somewhere, like the Maldives. Maybe one of those cute, beach villa type accommodations jutting out into the sea? I so wanted to do that for our honeymoon. I had it all planned – get married in Sri Lanka and honeymoon on a beach in the Maldives. We didn't do that of course, since my ex insisted on everyone from his family being invited, from forty times removed Aunty Betty, to the cousins he had never met and would never meet again after the wedding.

Weddings suck up money faster than I can eat a bag of M&S toffees. If I get married again, it'll be a little garden party for family and friends and me and my guy escaping to Portofino for a lovely romantic getaway, or perhaps a long weekend trip to the vineyards of Bordeaux? Wine has become such a special part of my life over the past few months that I might as well get more intimately acquainted with the stuff!

Please God may I get married again one day? I've always wanted to go to Portofino!

<u>7.20 p.m.</u>
Oh no! I just realised that I can't meet James on that date this Saturday. Lockdown killed off dating, then easing of restrictions gave us hope and now the tiers are crushing that hope and grinding it back into the ground. That's it, life is poo and I am now naming a number two a BJ.

<u>Midnight (again)</u>
I feel so sad about the restrictions coming. I have this horrible impending feeling of zoom permeating through me. Anxiety levels slowly rising today but couldn't show kids. Ate a lot from the snack cupboard, much to the dismay of the kids who were also hoping to empty said cupboard.

Must fight the doom and gloom. Back to the meditations and the affirmations.

Blimey! My resolution and affirmation wall is full! That says a lot about the past seven months!

I AM A SURVIVOR AND I SO GOT THIS!

Will add that one tomorrow. Too tired to get out of bed and add to the wall... Oh boy, even saying the word 'wall' makes me think of Shirley Valentine. Can't believe I have become 2020's equivalent of Shirley flipping Valentine!!!

Thursday 15th October

I was having the best dream. I was sunbathing on a luxurious sun lounger on the edge of a Maldives beach villa overlooking a shimmering blue ocean. Waves gently lapped against the wooden stilts and that shlop, shlop sound created by the movement under the villa, was so calming. Yet the sound it was making, was also calling me away from this magical moment.

Shlop ...Shlop...

'Mum? Mum?' I got up off my sun lounger and looked around me quizzically. I was on a luxurious island. There was no one around, but still the call rung out extracting me from a delightful place that could only be described as heaven. Yet I could still hear the sound of the water hitting the wood of the village stilts underneath me.

Shlop!

'Mumma?' I sat up in bed. I wasn't in the Maldives after all, but in my bedroom. The room was dark and I could hear the rain pelting against the conservatory roof outside my window. I reached for my phone and squinted at the face to make out the time. Must find those glasses! 2.52 a.m. Whyyyyyyy? I get up and walk to where I am being called from – the bathroom.

Ben was sitting on the toilet, hair dishevelled, wearing nothing but his pants, which were sitting around his ankles. Same pants from yesterday and the day before. I heard another 'shlop' sound and recognised immediately, the sound I heard when I was lying in my bed in a half asleep state. Ben was having a poo.

'Why did you wake me Ben? It's so early.'

'I couldn't find the toilet paper and I wanted you to help me get some.'

'It's there. In your hand.' I say feeling exasperated and looking a tad confused. He rolls his eyes at me (*it's too early for this* I want to scream, but am way too tired to even do that).

'I know now…I found it attached to this note you wrote on the wall. Mum, what does it mean? I don't get it!'

I looked at the note in question, which stated in large black felt tip pen:

FROM NOW ON A POO IN THIS HOUSE IS TO BE KNOWN AS A BJ (BIG JOBBIE).

Signed The Queen.

Ah...that note. I forgot to mention last night Diary, that in utter dismay at once again losing work and my first date with anyone since the beginning of November last year being cancelled, that I may have consumed over half a bottle of Chardonnay. It was a very good half bottle though. Being tipsy and peed off, I deemed it highly funny to write the note. I am the queen of the house after all, so no reference at all to the real Majesty. And of course, no correlation with any one person in Parliament! On a side note, I wonder what the real Queenie calls her big jobbies?

I explained to Ben that that I thought it would be fun give our poo a new name. I should have known better. Ben, being a creatively minded boy, then spent the day re-naming many of the day-to-day activities in the house and writing notes everywhere to help remind us!

Mental note...tell Ben as little as possible about anything remotely controversial since his resulting actions could wind the heck out of his sister. Boredom is biting at her ankles and she is always on the verge of wanting to throttle someone. Can't imagine whom she takes after.
I decided to return to bed after the school drop off today. Tomorrow, my life is about to drastically change and I am not sure if it's for the better!

<u>5.30 p.m.</u>
Collected Saskia from London. The kids' dad took the other two out for a takeaway so I could go alone. I love these car journeys to collect her when it's just me. The head switch off time is so welcome. Although I also love spending time with Ben when he comes, he does prefer to stay home and play on his Xbox and Lily doesn't enjoying leaving the house much these days.

I do worry about how insular she is becoming. She keeps telling me how depressed and anxious kids her age are feeling. They need social interaction, the girls thrive on drama and gossip and hanging around with each other talking about boys, music, make up and clothes. Boys are missing their sports and park times. The kids all seem to be on their phones continuously scrawling through and checking on each other's social media Snapchat and TicTok stories. Their world is their phone and it cannot be healthy going forward.

What else do they have? School is no longer fun and is full of restrictions. They wear masks in corridors, are not allowed to touch each other or pass others in the wrong direction. There are door monitors on some classrooms watching to see if they are adhering to the rules. They cannot bring in books or papers or use the school's equipment. It's more like a prison environment than school. No wonder so many of them are depressed, anxious and suicidal.

Gosh, what sad thoughts to go to bed with. Right now, I could watch *Moana* with S, but she's having girly times with her sis in Lily's room. I'll stick on a guided meditation next to my pillow and go to sleep that way. It's helped before and I'm sure it will work again. Though I must confess, that thoughts of tomorrow are filling my head more than they should. Must sleep. Must sleep!

Friday 16th October

Whilst the kids were in school, Saskia and I went to collect the puppy. It was a long drive, but we blasted music and chatted whilst stuck in two lots of motorway traffic.

On the way home, she sat in the back with this cute, adorable ball of blond Labrador fluff. We stopped to buy some puppy food, a blanket and a couple of toys at the big pet shop near the breeder. Typically, the pet food that the puppy has been fed on since birth, was from a pet shop brand that only last month, moved out of our town; yet another casualty of lockdown. Our little market town is full of empty shops and many with 'Closing Down' signs splayed across their windows. Some were struggling before March, but this has been one of the many sad results of the lockdowns and that's just the street facing shops, never mind the countless number of small businesses and self employed who rely on footfall to keep going. I fear we will be seeing the negative affects economically for many years to come.

We got home and then we waited for their dad to bring Ben back from school. It was all planned. The girls knew, but we agreed to keep it a surprise for Ben.

He walked in the door and this fluff ball ran straight to him. Ben, looking both bemused and in total shock, bent down, picked him up and burst into tears. And suddenly, my fears about taking on the responsibility of a puppy, crumbled. It wasn't about me; it was all about them. They needed this distraction; they needed this little bundle of joy to give their love to, when so much had been taken away from them.

In that moment, I saw a slither of the purpose of my life as a mother – to give joy, hope, guidance, security, love, nurture and also encouragement. I had to encourage and coax them out of the mental pitfalls of this lockdown situation, with everything I could muster within my mortal, motherly means. And if that meant bringing a puppy into our home, then so be it.

'Oh he's just had a poo on the carpet! Oh no, he's got it on his feet and he's running around the living room. Mum?'

It's for the good of the kids Pen, the good of the kids…

<u>Midnight</u>

Many poos and wees later. I am exhausted. As soon as I cleaned one up, there seemed to be another. And tonight I am sleeping on the sofa in the living room next to his puppy size crate. He is howling to be cuddled and I am pining for sleep. I know it's going to get better. I know it will. Just have to get through the next two weeks of puppy toilet and sleep training hell.

And they decided on a name for him finally – Jimbo. I once had a university friend called Jimbo. Jumbo Jimbo the girls nicknamed him. Cannot imagine why?

Tuesday 20th October

Puppy training is getting there. He's started going outside for number two's, but we still have the odd accident. That poor carpet; it used to be beige. I've littered the downstairs with bed wetting mats. But he seems to prefer to either peeing right next to one or just catching the edge. Argh.

I keep telling myself it will get better.

<u>7 p.m.</u>

Pulling my hair out! I was so exhausted, that I went upstairs to have a little catch-up nap. Jimbo was cuddling with the kids downstairs whilst they watched a film after dinner. All was good in the land of the Woods. I was just drifting off when I could hear a commotion from below. Ben and Lily were always bickering, which is what I could hear, so I ignored them. It ascended to non-ignorable levels though and I ended up shouting down asking what the heck was going on.

'Jimbo's had a poo and walked it all over the living room!' came the less than wonderful reply. I groaned. Not only did I not have my craved for nap, but I now had to go downstairs and scrub puppy poo out of the carpet.

I was just about to go down when Lily kindly shouted up 'Stay in bed Mum, I'll do it. You need a rest.' Aw, I love Lily. She is always doing things like this for me. She may moan like a typical teenager, want to always throttle her brother for being annoying, stay in her room, snack all day long and never go to bed before 1 a.m., but the kid has a heart of gold.

I snuggle back into bed with a sigh of relief and a happy smile on my face. Then in walks Ben to completely dismantle those happy thoughts. He jumped on my bed and my nose immediately crinkled in disgust.

'You smell of poo,' I declared flaring my nostrils at him.

'Oh cheers Mum! And there's me coming to say hello.'

'No Ben, you really do smell of poo. Did Jimbo poo on you? It smells just like one of his.'

'No, don't be silly. How could he poo on me? Lily's cleaning up his poo downstairs. You should have seen it Mum, it was EVERYWHERE!'

'Wait. Did you step in it?' I eyeballed his socks. The ones that were on my clean, freshly put on the night before, white duvet. One of them had a brown smudge stain on the bottom of his right foot. 'You've got poo on your sock Ben!' I screamed in dismay.

'No I haven't' he said in defiance. Then he looked underneath his socked feet. 'Oh!' he declared in horror as he saw the smelly stain.

'Ben take your socks off now and throw them onto the floor!' I shouted in dismay. My duvet… my heart was sobbing even if my face was not declaring the tears yet.

I ordered him to strip off and jump in the shower. Smelly boy. Then I checked everywhere he had walked. Yep, there was the evidence – all up the stairs and into my room. The duvet needed stripping. I sighed in exasperation. Ben apologised. What could I do?

What I always do…took a deep breath, rolled up my sleeves and got on with it.
I may also have cursed a little under my breath for quite a while and then grabbed a large glass of something white and cold from the fridge, but otherwise, I think I handled it just fine.

Friday 23rd October

Would you Adam and Eve it? James from the dating site wants to meet up for a walk somewhere and a takeaway coffee. He said he would drive to me and we could get to know each other via social distancing.

Sounds bliss. But I had to turn him down.

I have a puppy now. My dating life for the foreseeable future is over, at least for the next five to six weeks anyway. Sigh. You couldn't make this up!

On a positive note, Matt is back on the delivery route. Apparently he had a couple of weeks of acting work. Good for him. I think he's quite keen too, since he really should have been in more of a rush to deliver the rest of his packages, instead of cooing on the doorstep stroking my puppy.

Hah...now that's fuel for a pleasant dream this evening!

Thursday 29th October

Ben turned ten today. The rule of six is in place, so his dad is taking him and three friends paintballing on Saturday, along with Saskia who is sometimes more boy than girl. Lily being very girly, grimaced at the idea of being painfully splattered with paintballs. I'm with Lily, so not my idea of fun. Anyway, I had to look after the puppy.

It's not cheap having a paintballing party, but his dad is paying thank goodness. Gutted not to have worked those days this month. Oh well. I'm sure things will change soon, or maybe not. Just heard that we may be heading into another month's lockdown on 5th November. That's the talk anyway but I really hope not, but if we are...bummer. Just hope the kids are remaining in school. It feels like they've only just got back. Lily has her mocks coming up and Ben is only just starting to make new friends. I need to restructure my working options so I can actually earn something whilst the kids are home/in lockdown/locked up.

Anyway, today is about Ben and it's his special birthday and I am going to make sure he has a lovely day no matter what. He got a BMX bike plus loads of lovely bits from the rest of us. And he has a puppy. What more could a ten year old want?

Monday 2nd November

Three more days left until lockdown number 2. I feel the need to do something crazy beforehand. Like celebrating with friends the night before, and drinking too much alcohol and maybe go mad and dance on a table? Or perhaps run around the cul-de-sac naked or something equally drastic! Okay, I wouldn't do that unless I had a very near perfect body, which I don't have. I'm not as flappy clappy as I was, but I still wouldn't want the world to see me naked. Which reminds me - my 76 year-old neighbour still can't look me in the eye, especially as it wasn't my eyes that caught his attention! Oh Lordy!

Spoke to Matt today when he delivered another parcel. Lily keeps on buying. Go Lily, go Lily! Hah.

On a positive note, Jimbo has finally cracked the toilet training. Apart from the odd wee in the corner of the training mat still, he now knows that the garden is his toilet and not the living room carpet. I feel we are moving forward. One step back into lockdown and one step forward for my fur mummy sanity!

Wednesday 4th November

I tried Diary, I really tried to get out locally tonight. But alas, there were no takers since most of my friends are isolating either for themselves or for partners or parents. Most of my main social life is in London and with the kids home, going to the city tonight, wasn't ever going to happen. Last thing I would want is to get stuck in London on the start of lockdown!

Oh boy, I really do have the saddest social life. It's okay though, because I can honestly say that I am not alone... hah, no pun intended. I can actually be quite funny without even trying.

11.30 p.m.
Made the kids watch *Moana* with me. I swear I have seen this at least ten times since this lockdown began in March. I still cried, laughed and sang in all the right places. I think the sneaky, double measure gin o'cocktail helped a lot. The way I reasoned it, if I were out with friends tonight, I would have had more than one large drink. Especially if I knew a month of national lockdown was coming the next day.

I am feeling so tearful right now. Mustn't show the kids, so saving it for my private moments with you Diary.

Damn it – that really sounds so weird. Penelope Shirley Valentine is now my new name. Could be worse, it could be Penelope Carole Baskin. She definitely did it. Not that I care, or was standing for half hour over Lily's shoulder as she binge watched episode after episode tonight. I swear that programme is more addictive that M&S toffees! Though maybe not...

Thursday 12ᵗʰ November

A week into lockdown and already life feels like Groundhog Day. My exciting days consist of taking kids to school, fussing over the dog, trying not to eat, looking out the window for the DPD van (so sad that my levels of excitement have come to that), food shopping, doing the online screenwriting course I am running out of enthusiasm for, because my enthusiasm for doing anything at all, is diminishing more and more each day. I need to shake my life up a bit. But how the hell do I do that?

I called David.

'I'm losing the will,' I told him.

'That's because you have fallen into the fear trap.'

'Yes I can feel it. I do feel so fearful about the future, work, my kids, lockdowns, when this will all end, or IF it will end.' I started to cry. I couldn't help myself.

'Look. There's nothing you can do about the past, so get out of the feelings of lack and being a failure. The future isn't written yet, so why worry about something that may or may not happen? Okay?'

'Okay?' I respond with a sniffle, wiping the mush from my nose and eyes.

'So,' David continued, 'let's take a lot at the present moment. You can do something about that.'

'I can? How?'

'By the way you react to it. Look, there's nothing you can do about what's going on outside of your own direct world. But how you react to it you can control. If you want to stay in bed and watch TV all day, then do it. If you want to eat crap food and drink a bottle of wine every night, then do it. But is it going to benefit you in any way shape or form?'

I hesitated on my answer as I had been doing quite a bit of this and despite justifying it to myself, I knew it wasn't making me feel happy. 'No I guess not.' I finally replied.

'So you have a choice. We always have a choice. If you want to take away your choice, then continue living in fear. It might cover your eyes for a little while, but it won't blind you completely. The truth will still exist, whether you choose to see it or not.'

I had to ponder on this for a few moments. His words were profound and kicked me right where it hurt – my sub-conscious.

'So...' I ventured, 'I can choose exactly how I want to feel and what I want to believe right?' David agreed. 'But if I continue with fear, I live in a perpetual state of worry, anxiety and stress and not knowing if I am coming or going? Or if I let go and trust the process, I could live a much happier life? Am I getting that right?'

'Yes pretty much. But think of it this way. If you always live in fear, the vibrational state you exist in, will keep you living in a low mood, with low energy and always feeling like pants quite truthfully. But if you choose to raise your vibration by feeling happy, calm, at peace and trusting, then you raise your vibration to higher levels and naturally start to feel happier. You will also inadvertently affect those around you because your energy will transfer onto them and your environment.'

'Oh I see now. Wow! That's fascinating. Can we really affect others through our energy or vibe?' I asked incredulous.

'Of course! Remember, *your vibe attracts your tribe.*'

I thanked David for his time and wisdom. What he said made perfect sense. It was true about not being able to have control over the past or the future, but that I could control the present by choosing how to let it affect me. Gosh, all that meditation and self-development I had been doing over the past eight months, has really helped me to see things differently. It's helped me to cope if I am being honest. I have been less judgemental, more hopeful and more open to possibility and opportunity. It's only been this last lockdown that I have felt so lost and low within myself. The first lockdown I had Saskia with me, and it felt very much like a holiday. Then I had the other two at home, which distracted me, plus the weather was so good. This time, it's me and a puppy.

Friday 13th November

Friday 13th and I woke up sweating buckets. I dreamt about being on a beach with Boris and my belly was bigger than his.

New resolutions:

I WILL LOSE MY BELLY BEFORE SUMMER COMES
I WILL NOT IN ANYWAY RESEMBLE THE PM

I won't be able to see my wall if I keep adding new resolutions. Must remember to actually recite my affirmations and resolutions more often, or at least look at them. My wall... so not going to mention that woman's name!

Saturday 14th November

Can't believe it! Matt asked for my number today. Wow. I had a feeling he liked me, but didn't expect that. Seems there is a Cupid out there and she shot an arrow straight into the ass of my DPD man. How wonderful!

4.45 p.m.

Kids and I are bored of lockdown. We're all grating each other's last nerve. It's only been 2 weeks. With the puppy growing bigger everyday and us on top of each other, the house is feeling like we are living in a tightly closed oyster shell. We literally can't breathe. Thankfully Jimbo gets his last injection on Monday, so we can finally take him out. Praise God for small mercies!

I wonder if Matt has a dog? If he does, we could go for walks together. How romantic. Will have to wait until after lockdown, but the idea of walking together sounds bliss. I wonder when he will call? Pen get a grip! You only gave him your number at midday and he's working. He'll call when he's ready to!

Am I really now having an argument with myself and writing it up in my Diary? Has my life become that miniscule that I debate stuff in my own bloody Diary? Oh boy!

I'm a lockdown mum, get me out of here!!!

9.50 p.m.
Ben in bed. Jimbo asleep and Lily and I watching a film snuggled together in our PJs, munching on Tyrells Sea Salt and Vinegar crisps and a big bar of Cadbury's. I really don't like the sweet taste of Cadbury's, but since it's the only chocolate in the house and I have my period, it will definitely suffice.

My phone pings under my bottom on the sofa. It's Matt. I message back. He messages immediately and then so do I. This goes on for about ten minutes before Lily sighs heavily and I send a 'gotta go' message.

Tonight I went to bed with a smile on my face: first time for quite a while.

Sunday 22ⁿᵈ November

We've survived 2.5 weeks of lockdown number 2 so far. It feels like forever. On my own with just the puppy as the kids are at their dad's. Kicking around with the screenwriting idea, but I have lost inspiration. Had to escape the house so went to the shops.

I had just paid for the groceries, when I had the biggest urge to sneeze. I kept holding it in until just at the exit. I was just about to take off my mask when two old ladies and another couple walked in. At that exact moment, the most patient sneeze on the planet just ran out of patience.

Aitchoooo!!!!

Sneezing in your mask is not a fun experience. But at least I didn't spray four people...just my face! Gross.

Matt messaged me this evening. How lovely to finally have someone to chat with. He asks me lots of questions about myself, which shows he is interested, but truthfully, I have a strange feeling that he isn't telling me the full story about himself. Every time I ask a searching question about his ex, his kids or dating, he quickly diverts the line of conversation back to me. So I also try to hold back from telling him too much, however, I am an open book and the lack of adult stimulation for the past few months, means I tend to give away more than I probably should. Must try to be a little more mysterious. I think it might make me more appealing and attractive.

Besides, if he is 'The One', then we will have plenty of time to get to know each other when we realise we are indeed perfectly compatible.

Blimey Diary, maybe I should skip all the polite preliminaries and go ahead and book the church and reception right now? Calling a guy I haven't even had a bleeding date with, 'The One'? Come on Pen!

Yet another new resolution for Penelope/Shirley wall:

I MUST GET A BLOODY LIFE

Saturday 28th November

My birthday and it's on a Saturday and there's nothing I can do except party on with the kids at home. In fact, it's been one of my best birthdays ever. My kids know me so well and I can honestly say that I am utterly grateful for my children.

Despite all that has happened this year and all that we have lost individually and as a family, I am so proud of my children and who they are becoming. S is building three sources of income, Lily has a little business going and started a part time job, as well as developing a talent for home made skin care recipes. And since I have become her guinea pig tester, my skin has never felt as good! The one involving vanilla tealeaves and honey was the most painful and messy, but boy did our faces glow afterwards!

Ben wants to run his own car cleaning company, but I told him he has to cut his entrepreneurial teeth on doing my battered and bruised car first! Funny, he isn't rushing to start the business anytime soon!

He has a great relationship with his dad. It's been funny watching them rock off to the park with their skateboards under their arms. My 49 year-old ex has re-discovered the boy in him and doing loops on the half pipe thingy in the skate park. Ben loves it (too young to be embarrassed yet) and it's had such a deepening impact on the connection between the two of them.

Oh and I got a happy birthday message from Matt. Yay. That made my day! Plus one from that scoundrel of an ex-boyfriend Richard, which I did not respond to. He had his moment and blew it.

On the whole Diary, despite everything, I have so much to be grateful for.

Monday 30th November

Huge, beautiful bouquet of flowers delivered to my door at lunchtime. No note, which really threw me. I messaged all the possible suspects, but it wasn't them. There were only two guys left to choose from – Matt and Richard. Both threw me into a quandary.

If it was Matt, which seemed less likely since we have only just started messaging and nothing romantic, then I had to ask myself why he would be sending a woman he has only just met, only just started messaging and never actually as much as touched her cardigan, let alone hold her hand, an obviously expensive bouquet to her door? Being a delivery guy though, it kind of makes sense that he would go down that route. Hah, 'route'... honestly, I surprise myself sometimes!

If, on the other hand, it was Richard, who earns a fortune and who often used to send me gifts like this (out of guilt I can now assume?), then why, after a year of not being together, would he be doing this gesture? What would his motivation be? The only messages I have received from him since the split, were a day after when he apologised and then back in April asking me if I was managing. He would have guessed I had lost my income streams. There was also, the birthday message on Saturday from him.

Diary, if it is Richard then what's his game plan? I know he would have one; he's that type of guy! Then again, if it is Matt, but he didn't leave a note, then how the heck am I supposed to respond? I can't thank him for flowers if he didn't get me any. That would be like rubbing his nose in it for forgetting my birthday. And damn awkward explaining that someone else is interested enough to send me a bouquet.

Am I overthinking this Diary? Should I just enjoy the flowers and not mention it to Matt and see what happens? Oh the problems of a middle-aged, single woman in lockdown! I must get a grip if this is all I have to worry about. At least lockdown has taken away most of my worries for now:

- I don't worry about looking for work since there isn't any and if there was I can't do it
- I don't have to worry about money since I have no possible or potential income at present and I know I am broke (mustn't say 'broke' according to the speaker Les Brown – I have a 'cash flow challenge')
- I don't have to worry about fitting into any of my work clothes since there is no work

- I don't have to wear make up, brush my hair, wear a bra or even get out of my PJs if I don't want to. Unless of course there is a DPD delivery due!
- The kids are all safe and Lily and Ben are in school and not homeschooling. Yay!

On the face of it, I'm doing okay really.

<u>11 p.m.</u>

No messages from either Matt or Richard. What if it's not them and someone else? Should I be excited or worried that I have forgotten to thank someone for the flowers? What if there really was a note and I accidentally threw it away? Damn, that really could be a possibility. Will rummage through the bin tomorrow.

Gosh, I must stop overthinking everything through. I wonder if other people are like me? I swear I have got ten times worse since the lockdowns began. New resolution (don't think it's up there, but can't see as I have so many written down):

I WILL NOT OVERTHINK EVERYTHING

I AM A LAID BACK PERSON

I ACCEPT FLOWERS NO MATTER WHO SENDS ME THEM

Wednesday 2nd December

End of lockdown. Thank Flip for that!!! Blimey, I felt that one.

Okay now back to reality and some form of normality. We don't know how long this one will last, so it's every man, woman and child for themselves fighting for basic freedoms! Well, I would, but I was mad enough to get a puppy and then lose all my paid work. I have found a dog walker/sitter though, so when the work does come in, I have someone local to help.

Lily's GCSE Mock exams have started and so there's more stress at home and lots of driving her to and from her exams. It's the only way I could persuade her to do them. Life is tough for kids right now and especially for teenagers. They live on social interaction; it's everything to them and it's so unhealthy for them to stay holed up in their bedrooms all day and all night, only crawling out like moles to forage for food. Their feeling of helplessness is real. They do more research than most of us older people do, and so they are often that much more aware of the situation that we give them credit for. If I want a non-media point of view of the virus and a different narrative than the one we are given, then I go to my girls. I love that they are so open-minded. I've learned a lot from my kids over the past few months. It's a shame the teens think the nation is blaming them for the spread of this flipping virus. As if they haven't got enough to deal with simply trying to keep sane!

Mind you, the puppy is helping her emotionally deal with everything. Plus she has taught him a new trick – she spits fruit out of her mouth and he jumps and catches it in his. Not sure if I should clap or groan at this one!

<u>7.45 p.m.</u>
Received a message from Matt asking if I liked the flowers. Wow! They were from him. I'm in shock. I didn't realise he liked me *that* much. He asked if we could go for a coffee sometime. Am I allowed Diary? And why am I asking you? I definitely need more friends...

151

Thursday 3rd December

I thought I had killed myself today Diary.

The conservatory leaks water from condensation. The non-condensing tumble dryer doesn't help either despite having a tube sucking the damp out via a cat flap. Puppy was bored and nicking shoes and toys and running with them outside into the rain, hoping to be chased. I was distracted finishing some coursework after dinner and kids were watching a film. We were all pretty chilled really.

Then out of the corner of my eye, I saw Jimbo grab Ben's new trainer shoe, dart into the conservatory and was just about to run outside, since the doors were open. He stood there looking at me and waiting, since for him, this was a new game. I jumped up and ran after him to stop the shoe going outside, but the floor was covered in water. My legs flew into the air and I landed with a huge crack on the back of my head. I screamed a blood-curdling scream that sent the kids rushing over in full panic mode.

'The floor is wet, be careful!' I cried with my supposedly dying breath.

Lily was in shock. I would normally be calm in times of crisis, but I honestly thought I was going to die since the crack was so loud. I guess a part of me wanted to say goodbye to them whilst I could. How dramatic! The part of my head that hit the floor was throbbing. It was such a huge sounding crack. I was sure I had split my head open. I told Lily to call 111 immediately. They helped me upstairs into my bed since Jimbo kept bouncing over me and licking my face. Guilt kisses no doubt! My bed - a good place to die in case the ambulance didn't arrive in time. You could tell I was thinking rationally! Lily went to grab some frozen peas, but I hadn't been shopping yet and all we had were frozen raspberries. They are definitely not as flexible and kind on throbbing bumps as peas!

Lily found the source of the crack that I'd heard on my head. Thankfully it wasn't my skull but a hard plastic hairclip, which had fallen from the top of my head down to the very position I landed on. It probably saved me from serious damage to my head. Yes I had a bruised, cut and very swollen lump, mainly from the hairclip it must be said, but I was going to live another day. The responder on 111 agreed also and so no hospital admission was required.

At least I got to stay in bed for the rest of the evening, was totally fussed over and got to watch *Notting Hill* on Lily's laptop. She even brought me up a cup of tea. First time in such a very long time I had tea in bed! Not sure how I will be able to sleep tonight though – frozen shoulder on left and bumpy, painful head on the right. But at least I was going to be uncomfortable, in pain and not able to sleep in my own, glorious bed.

Diary, the lengths a mother has to go to, to get an early evening in bed and a cuppa made for her!

Saturday 5th December

No kids today and I locked the puppy in his crate for two hours to escape to a nearby larger town to buy Christmas bits for the kids. I have 45 minutes of driving, split two ways, time to park and allowance for queuing for the car park. That left me around one hour to fit in a whole day's worth of shopping. Mmm, I didn't plan this getting a puppy thing near Christmas very well did I?

So, there I was, rushing from one shop to the next, when I saw a familiar face in the crowd. It was Matt. And he wasn't alone. He had his arm around a very attractive brunette and the way he was looking at her, it was obvious that she wasn't his sister! I felt the blood drain from my face and curdle in my stomach. I hid behind a large man walking in front of me, peeking my face from behind his left arm every so often so I could keep an eye on my suspect philanderer. They walked into the coffee shop I had planned to get a hot chocolate from, just as the man in front of me turned around to scowl at me for being a little close. I'm sure I stayed 2 metres away, but he could obviously hear my heart beating like church bells inside my chest.

'Bastard!'

'I beg your pardon?' said the man in front of me, fully facing me now and glaring down with a look that would have withered a lesser soul. I hadn't realised I had spoken that aloud. That was meant to be a head thought about Matt, but I guess too long talking to myself at home means I can't tell if I am thinking or speaking my words any longer!

'Oh sorry, not you! I was listening to an audible book in my ear. I get so involved with the story. This guy was caught two-timing his girlfriend and I must have just let slip my thoughts. Sorry.' I have become a solid liar. Since when did that happen? Who the heck am I becoming? Thankfully I had my earpiece in as I was listening to some meditation music to calm me down as I darted in and out of queue laden shops, flipping my mask on and off like the performance of a quick striptease act.

'Ah' said the guy with a nod whose face softened into an engaging smile. I could tell he was about to start a conversation with me, since his mouth was open and about to launch, but I wasn't feeling up for a conversation with a stranger today, so I made an excuse and darted into the nearest shop.

The guys in the barber's shop I walked into all looked up at me, as did the three men having their hair cut. It was a very small shop and the sign on the front door that I hadn't of course looked at, said 'Please wait outside to be called in. Appointments only.'

'Er...I...sorry, I thought you were Greggs. I fancied a sausage roll.' Who says that? In a barber's shop? I escaped quicker than you could say 'Nutter woman!' and I swear I heard an eruption of laughter follow me out. Mortified, saddened and angry, I decided to go home. Before I left, I did try taking a sneaky peek inside the coffee shop Matt and the woman entered, but they had already left. Exhaling a deep sigh (behind a mask), I went in, ordered a hot chocolate, with extra cream, marshmallows and a more than generous sprinkling of chocolate dust. I was broken hearted and felt dismembered by the disappointing behaviour of yet another user loser. Today I needed as much fat and sugar as I could get my lips on.

12.40 a.m.

No one could blame me for drinking three glasses of wine by myself tonight. I've been so good lately and even lost 2 kilos. Tonight I ate everything I shouldn't and drank more than I should. Sod the kilos. No message from Matt either. And Richard sent me another message saying I hope I enjoyed my birthday. Now I am not sure if it was Matt who sent the flowers or Richard. Oh man!!!

Diary, why is even non-dating dating so bleeding complicated? ☹

Tuesday 8ᵗʰ December

Matt messaged me earlier. I aired him (on Lily's advice). So one minute I am getting expensive bouquets of flowers from him (I think) and him asking for a real date, then the next he's walking with his arm around another woman looking into her eyes as if she was the most beautiful thing on the planet. Then he forgets I exist for four days, until he finally remembers his little 'delivery bit on the side' and thinks a little 'Hi beautiful, how are you doing?' text is going to send me drooling all over him!

I don't bloody think so!

Midnight (ish)
Diary, the trouble with airing a guy when you like them, is the constant checking of your phone to see if:
1. they've read your message
2. if they've messaged back
Argh. This dating lark is so hard and I'm not even dating the guy! I'm 48 years of age. I should have all this sorted by now. Get a grip Pen, get a bleeding grip!

Wednesday 9ᵗʰ December

I temporarily forgot Matt is a delivery driver. There I was in my really scruffy paint covered jeans and daughter's too small crop top that barely covers my boobs let alone my belly, painting the upstairs hallway. I was blasting Take That from my laptop and bellowing way out of pitch to *Relight my Fire*. I thought I heard my front door bell ring just as I was singing along to the line, 'Your love is my only desire,' really loud and out of tune. I stopped and listened. Silence. I resumed the singing. This time a loud knock at the door and the puppy, who had been asleep in his cage, suddenly started barking.

I wasn't expecting anyone, so dashed downstairs.

'Hi!' Matt stood at the door with a parcel. I was wearing not a scrap of make up, so my eyes were beady and my lashes virtually transparent since they are so light. I was holding a paintbrush in my left hand, which I forgot about and out of habit, wiped a hair from my face with said paintbrush. It was still wet with paint.

Matt chuckled and held his hand to his face in shock, as paint swept across my left cheek and eye and up into my pulled back hair, which earlier that morning, had started its life neatly piled on the top of my head, but after an hour of painting, some of it with my head almost upside down, my hair had fallen in a slump over the left side of my head. So that too received much of the paint.

'Oh dear!' he said with a laugh. I was mortified.

'I've been painting.' Really? Dur..., of course I'd been painting. And now I had painted myself also.

'I can see that,' he said still laughing. 'You're so funny Penny.'

He called me Penny. I liked that. Come on Pen, he's an actor, don't be fooled by his charm. I admonished myself despite feeling myself blushing (not that you could tell under the white paint) and smiling.

'You didn't reply to my text. Did you get it?' he asked. I squirmed.

'I've been a bit busy. Sorry.' I lied.

'That's ok. So are you still up for grabbing that coffee sometime?'

I thought for a moment and despite how I looked, I decided to be truthful. The old me would have said yes immediately and kicked myself later for not playing harder to get.

'I saw you the other day,' I started, 'I was doing some Christmas shopping and saw you...with a woman. You looked kinda like an item.' Brave Pen, very brave.

I watched Matt's face as he stood there in deep thought. Then his expression lightened and he declared, 'Oh you mean when I was with Helen my ex wife?'

His ex wife?

My face must have looked a picture because he quickly told me how she was having a tough time with their oldest son who was going off the rails with lockdown. He'd fallen in with a couple of older boys who weren't a good influence on him. He didn't mention in which way, so I could only guess at drugs or alcohol maybe?

'Oh. I see, but why would you have your arm around her and the way you were looking at her suggested you were a couple. Bit awkward to be going for a coffee with you if you're already in a relationship.' Who is this brazen me? Go on Pen!

He stood there for a moment and contemplated me. Not the situation, but me. I suddenly felt totally exposed, naked in his presence: tummy compromised and half covered in paint!

'Pen, I like you. You're funny and different.' I think he was referring to my appearance with the 'different' bit. Inwardly I squirmed, especially thinking of his very stunning and immaculately dressed ex-wife.

'Hand-on-heart, I *am* single. I just have a special relationship with Helen. We care very much about each other and of course, we are tied because of the kids, but we could never be together. We're totally incompatible. She's like a best friend really. But I'd still love to have a coffee with you if you would like to have one with me, but I would I understand if you'd prefer not to?'

'Okay,' I said without another thought. 'Message me when. Gotta go now and scrub some paint off me before I harden.'

'Hah!' Matt chuckled as I quickly dodged behind the front door. *Harden? Oh my gosh Penny, you are just too much sometimes!*

As soon as I was safely behind the door and stopped admonishing myself, I screamed 'YES. GO ON PENELOPE WOOD! GET IN THERE!' as loud as I could. Jimbo by now was barking his head off. I was just about to run upstairs and scrub the paint off my face, when there was another knock on the door. I opened it sheepishly and there stood Matt with my parcel. Did he hear me? Oh Lordy, please say he didn't.

'I forgot to give you this,' he said with a wink as he handed me my box. He looked ready to burst into laughter any moment. Of course he heard me, how could he not? I think the whole bloody cul-de-sac heard me! Mortified is too kind a word for how I felt at that moment.

'Er...thanks,' I said as I received the box, quickly closed the door and rushed inside. Was it my imagination, but did our fingers touch?

<u>11.45 p.m.</u>
Diary, if Matt only knew what was in that box: a replacement BOB. A single girl's gotta do what a single girl's gotta do. Maybe I won't be single for long though? Lockdown's going to end soon enough, right?

Saturday 12th December

Told a friend about my accident caused by the flood in the conservatory and she gave me her condenser dryer today. She had a new kitchen and new appliances, so it was going spare. Result! I will pass on mine as soon as I can get some time to take a picture and post it out. Love the community spirit that has built up in our town and surrounding villages, because of the restrictions. I love that so many people are helping each other out. Restores my faith in humanity Diary. Shame the country's leaders couldn't be more philanthropic, especially when it seems there is so much cronyism and indecisive decision-making being dished out. I may not understand politics, maths or technical stuff, but I do recognise how differing humanity can be.

Thank you Universe for the kind and unselfish people in my life.

Monday 14th December

My production work has cancelled due to the Tiers. Three days work would have been the equivalent of 2 weeks of income needed to cover Christmas, from food shopping to presents. I am already just scraping by. I manage to pay my bills and credit cards, but I only pay the bare minimum. I guess at least they are being paid? Thankfully I was asked to write another article, so I will be paid for three by Friday. It will cover me just. I have also sold some books, which will cover Christmas lunch. Wow, I don't know when things have gone to the bare bones for us in such a long time.

I am so blessed with the children though. Their Christmas lists were humble this year. I feel so sad, but they don't need the burden of my worries on their shoulders. Truthfully though, I am really not that worried. I have a feeling that everything will be okay. What's that saying by John Lennon?

'Everything will be okay in the end, if it's not okay, it it's not the end.'

10.30 p.m.
Been feeling anxious all day worrying about money and the future. Going to do some extra praying tonight Diary. Now is not the time to lose my faith. I have to trust that everything will work out just as it is meant to. I refuse to give in to fear and worry.

If all else fails, there's always gin and toffees!

161

Tuesday 15th December

Blimey, God works quickly. £100 cash in an envelope through my door with a note in a handwriting I didn't recognise, saying:

'Thought you could use this to help with Christmas. Don't sweat the small stuff ☺'

I am not even going to consider who it could be. I am just going to say 'Thank you Universe' and gratefully accept it. That was definitely the quickest answer to prayer I have ever received.

Lily finished her Mock exams today. How I managed to get her to do them was a miracle in itself. Now to get her to do her college applications sorted for next September. She hasn't been a huge fan of school it must be said. And I have a date planned with Matt for when the restrictions are eased over the Christmas period. Actually going out to a restaurant with him and it's a surprise. This is the BEST day ever!!!

Saturday 19th December

Life, but not as we know it...

Bugger, shit and fannyflaps. We are now in Tier 4 and looks like Christmas freedom is off too! Boo-flipping-hoo! No night out in London for cocktails and a meal with Saskia and no date with Matt.

I lost the costume work on New Year's too, since it's been cancelled due to restrictions.

And today all the non-essential shops had to close so my books can't be sold in my friends' shops. It's a good job Lily and I went shopping two days ago or we wouldn't have got most of the presents I needed. She's been so organised this year unlike me. She's the reason I have seen Matt as often as I have. I'll be seeing him quite a lot next week too, since I have at least five presents still to get. Guess I will be back to online ordering tonight then!

This is going to be the weirdest Christmas. I must really try to make it special for the kids despite everything. At least they get to spend a week at their dad's. I wonder how Jimbo will react to just my face at home with him?

Argh. Life is so weird Diary. I sometimes wish I was a book, so someone else could write my life instead of me.

Did I really say that? Must stay off the gin, it's making my brain doolally.

Monday 21st December

I've lost my favourite and only fitting jeans. Can't find them anywhere. What the heck? It's the smallest house and nobody visits. Also can't find two of Ben's favourite joggers. How can I lose clothes? I think I am losing the plot, or on the change, or something. I burst into tears three times today. Kids are giving me a wide berth.

I don't want to adult anymore. Just saying…

Wednesday 23rd December

I forgot to get the turkey earlier! Now that everyone is forced to be home and not able to eat out or visit family, there isn't the surplus of food there normally is at this time of year. I had to wait for half an hour in a queue for M&S, since the queues for the other two supermarkets were round the corner and half way down the street! As a result, I ended up spending a third more on dinner than I would have. So grateful to my secret friend for that gifted money; I still don't know who it was.

I have been blessed this year in so many ways:
- My phone died last month and a friend gave me theirs when they upgraded their contract
- Two contacts agreed to sell my books in their shops (despite both having to close due to the Tiers)
- My Mac and printer both had issues and a friend of a friend came and helped me reconnect them
- My ex gave me an extra £150 maintenance for Christmas presents
- I sold five paintings this year
- I published my first novel and covered all my costs as well as made a few pounds profit
- I got given a condensing tumble dryer so my conservatory isn't going to be a death trap any longer
- My children and I are all safe and well and nobody I know has been very ill or died from the virus

So what if we don't have a lot materialistically, or much money, or that I have little work, or that the dates planned over the past month with the only two guys remotely interested in dating me, have both had to be called off due to Covid restrictions? So what? It means nothing in the grand scheme of life.

Diary, I shall eat chocolate, toffees, crisps and chips and not worry one iota this side of 2020. I will drink wine at 5.55 p.m. and pour myself a gin on a weeknight and not give a hoot. It's Christmas, and it's not the time to stress about excess or restrictions. Damn that was not a good choice of word. Bugger you 'rona for making life so hellishly crazy for most of 2020. Roll on 2021. I'm sure it's going to be better Diary, right? Right?

One day my friend, I know you will surprise me and answer me back.

Christmas Eve

I have all the kids at home. There is a real sense of excitement in the air. We all take the dog into the woods together and most of the time is spent in laughter. Unfortunately at my expense with the kids recalling all my strange foibles and habits and recounting my anecdotal stories (the ones where I don't come off so well), but hey, at least they were happy.

Having the kids around has been difficult for wrapping, so I've achieved this in spurts. I've even engaged the help of Jimbo – he has had to sit on rolls of paper whilst I cut them to fit the presents. He'll do anything for a treat!

Blimey, what a year it's been. And to think it started off so blinking well!

Christmas Day

The day has had it's ups and downs with sibling rivalry, but on the whole, it was a great day. No Christmas present complaints. Phew! Wine definitely helps if you start at 1 p.m. and only stop when you fall asleep watching a film on the sofa after lunch. Now that's what I call Christmas.

<u>10.45 p.m.</u>

Merry Christmas Diary. I'm zonked. It's a combo of early drinking and having so much to do. Sometimes I really feel being single, especially on special days like this. After all, there is only one of me to do everything. But at least the kids are happy and tomorrow evening they go off to their dad's for a week. I will miss them, but I will try to make the most of being alone and with the dog. We are both going to be pining a lot for the next few days.

Matt sent a short 'Hi, hope you are doing okay? Crazy time, but hope to catch up soon. Merry Christmas,' message yesterday. I sent him one today wishing him a Merry Christmas back. I wonder if we will ever meet up? I guess if I didn't see him most weeks delivering parcels, then this attraction between us would have fizzled out a while ago. It's exhausting this dating/non-dating lark.

Boxing Day

<u>10 p.m.</u>

Diary the house feels empty without the kids. I don't get it. One minute I am almost begging for peace and then, when I get it for a few days, I am missing them like mad. It's the same every single time they are away from me for more than a couple of days.

Perhaps it's because my life has shrunk so much over the past nine months? Most of the distractions that pulled me away from home and them, have disappeared. I rarely even drive the car, except to the shops, or to collect Saskia from London. I feel I live inside my head so much. If it wasn't for talking to Rosa, Andy or David on a regular basis, I would probably go insane. Like many of my connection friends, I've not heard from Jenni in a couple of months. But I think this time it's more about me not forcing the friendship and letting it go naturally. I feel fine about it too.

I feel the same about guys. I think about all the dates and flings I have had and how I tend to choose non-committal men. Richard said he was separated from his wife, but towards the end I was having doubts. One night, after too much gin, which I hadn't drank since I was eighteen, I confronted him about his marital status. He admitted that although he was effectively separated, he still lived with his wife of twenty-one years. We had been together for almost four months by this time. I was falling for the man and we spoke about a future together. To find out that I was the mistress, despite his claims that they hadn't slept together in over two years, was heart breaking. I felt he had denied me the right to choose. And I know I wouldn't have made the choice to be with him under those circumstances.

It's typical that once again I meet a man and we cannot even get a date sorted, since the bleeding government won't let us have one! He messaged me tonight. Said he is sad that we can't get together. It sounded like he was hinting at doing a naughty and meeting illegally. Mmm. Did I misread it? I think he's drunk. He's a bit soppy tonight. As long as he doesn't go down the dick pic route, I can deal with soppy.

Monday 28th December

Truthfully Diary, I'm actually loving my time alone. Until I get these headspace moments, I forget how much I crave it and how much it replenishes me. I know I am lucky to be able to have this time, unlike other women I know who don't have the same options as me.

With the kids away, the dog causes me the greatest stress though, as every single time I leave the living room where he spends his indoor life, he either barks like crazy or finds something of mine to chew. So far, I've lost a shoe, three pens and my favourite mascara to his boredom. He also has real separation anxiety issues. It's quite disconcerting when you have to go use the loo or grab something from upstairs, only to have a howling barrage of barking left behind you. I have super peed and super squeezed out a BJ more times in the past 2.5 months since this dog has arrived, than ever in my lifetime!

At least he is forcing me to relax and watch films. I refuse to watch most TV, though I do confess to enjoying a Sunday morning catch up with the Ellen Show, followed by a couple of episodes of the soothing melodious tones of that superb chef Rick Stein. He's good for me really so I guess he was a blessing for me as well as the kids.

11.45 p.m.
Must go to bed earlier. I did intend to this evening, but Matt kept messaging. I definitely think he's 'on heat', as his messages are building sexually. I am trying to stay off the alcohol whilst the kids are away and I know if I drink I might reciprocate. I really don't want to. I have a nagging feeling, possibly my instincts kicking in, that he isn't all he is making out to be. Truthfully, I've still not bought that excuse he gave me about his ex

wife. I don't doubt she is his ex wife, but the way he looked at her that day…I think he is still in love with her. And she is beautiful. If he is still in love with her, I couldn't compete with a beautiful ex wife who is also the mother of his kids.

Oh Diary, why is life so complicated? I haven't even started dating this guy and I'm contemplating breaking up with him. I didn't even get to have a snog. In fact, I haven't had a proper snog since last January!

New Year's Eve

<u>9.15 a.m.</u>

Not heard from Matt since I brushed off his sexual text advances on Monday. That's ok. I can handle it. I was really starting to like him too and was prone to enjoying a few fantasies in my head before sleep, but hey… not meant to be! There's always Brad to fall back on. Ooh, now I'm sure there's a dream to be had somewhere now Matt is no longer on the scene! Come on sub-conscious, you know you want to deliver me a Brad dream. Come to think of it, I haven't had any memorable dreams for a while. Wonder what that means?

<u>2.30 p.m.</u>

Kids back home in just two-days and Saskia is with her boyfriend. So it's just me and the Jimbo this New Year's Eve. Hope he likes Prosecco as I bought a bottle for the occasion? Hic. Just kidding Diary. Though I might spoil him with some slices of ham later.

Have just discovered *Bridgerton* on Netflix. I didn't think anything could match my two-day binge watching of *The Queen's Gambit* (so darn good), but this has kept me glued to my Mac for the past three hours. It's so addictive and I have already forgotten about Matt (Matt who?), since the leading male actor who plays the Duke, is so damn HOT. Oh my! I have the sweats and it isn't the onslaught of menopause. He is adorable, delicious and seductively charming all at once. Yummy.

<u>5 p.m.</u>

Okay, this is ridiculous, I have been watching this on and off (mostly on) since mid-morning. I've defrosted the freezer, cleaned and organised the food cupboards and even cleaned the bathroom. I couldn't justify watching it and not being productive. The Prosecco is helping a treat. I can honestly say, that this is one of the best New Year's Eve's I have had in ages. Is that sad Diary? Am I just a sad, middle-aged single mother binge watching Netflix on New Year's Eve? Er...yup!

<u>8.45 p.m.</u>

There's me thinking Matt has disappeared and then he messages me. Says he has been busy with the kids and this is the first chance he's had to message. He says he's missing me and hopes to grab a coffee in the New Year. Mmm. Not so sure. I'll have another Prosecco and message back then. I'm curious if nothing else.

<u>11.45 p.m.</u>

Coming to the last two episodes of *Bridgerton*. It's so good. I think I have sussed out who Lady Whistledown is, but I could be wrong. This is definitely the best NYE ever. In bed with the last of the Prosecco, messaging friends and family Happy New Year messages whilst binge watching this amazing series. I've had three old flames message, including Richard, and ignored them all to watch this fab programme. They stand no chance against the charms of the Duke. Hah. Neither would I come to think of it.

Love that my girls are older now so we can message at midnight on NYE. Love my children so much. Diary, it's going to be okay, I just know it. We'll soon be out of lockdown and back to living life to the full. I know I will have learned so much because of this. I prefer who I have become to who I was. I was so stressed all the time and anxious and chasing my tail constantly. I have more hope. Which given how much liberty and freedom I feel we've had taken from us, is the weirdest thing to say. I love this quote by the South African Archbishop Desmond Tutu:

'Hope is being able to see that there is light, despite all of the darkness.'

Diary, Matt messaged again, admittedly drunk. He sent the most bizarre text that made me smile but also sent me into a bit of a quandary (doesn't take much these days).

'Penny, you're so lovely. I wish I'd met you sooner. You are the type of woman I could easily fall for. Happy New Year. Love Matt xx'

'I could fall for you too Matt. Xx'

I shouldn't have texted back. I had drunk too much Prosecco on a near empty tummy and a couple of shots of tequila on a WhatsApp video with my Welsh mate. Sending that message straight back was a huge mistake! I should have waited. I just have this nagging feeling. I wish I hadn't messaged, but it's too late now. Bugger.

No reply back yet, so I am finally heading to sleep at 1.35am. *Bridgerton* is finished and I know who Lady Whistledown is and yes, I was right.

Friday 1st January 2021

I woke up with a stinking hangover and no lie in. What a joy to have a puppy the morning after New Year's Eve! 6.55am his inner alarm must have been set for. Argh. Why did I say yes to getting a dog? Whyyyyyy?

Anyway, at least I got out early on a dog walk. It was so beautiful and fresh this morning. Bloody freezing in fact. Couldn't find my gloves so my fingers were like frozen sausages when I got back home and my nose was pinker than a pig's bottom, though that could have been more to do with the booze the night before than the icy cold! That tequila – a gift from my next door neighbour at Christmas. Why did I open it at midnight? Thank goodness for Dry January. Never miss it and it'll soon sort me out. Though I think I might need drying out until spring, after the last 9 months of toxin abuse!

This is going to be my year. I can feel it. I don't care if it's started with restrictions and a lack of liberty. And a bleeding hangover. I don't care that I am not actually working and am barely keeping my head above the parapet. I don't even care that my life has more obstacles in front of me than a final round of the Krypron Factor. I just don't give a monkey's... THIS IS GOING TO BE MY YEAR!!

Bring it on!

And Diary, really not thinking about Matt's message from last night, or mine back: it's way too confusing. But have I misjudged him? Could he actually be 'The One'?

Saturday 2nd January

Kids home from their dad's today. Cupboards and fridge stocked, their beds made with fresh linen. Everything cleaned, dusted and tidied. I do this every weekend when the kids have been at his house. I love to start the week off on the right foot. I have to time to prepare, time to sort, clean and be psychologically prepared and relaxed. I sometimes buy flowers and often have fragrant candles in the living room – a welcome, homely return. So unlike a typical Sunday evening on my weekend. Then I am finishing the wine opened on Friday and disappearing upstairs for a two-hour escape bath time. The house is usually a built up mess and the cupboards are all but empty!

It was pretty exhausting watching them unpack all their gifts. But I love to see them happy. We watched a film and cuddled up together. After saying goodnight, I ran a bath to unpack myself also.

Not sure what 2021 is going to bring us but at least the kids are back to school on Monday. Halleluiah!!!

Sunday 3rd January 2021

YESSSSSSS!!!!!! The kids are back at school tomorrow! Whoop whoop! I adore them. I love them. I miss them dearly at times (I do, honest!), but...the thought of having my daytime space back and having the option to work again, fills me with so much joy! Happy days are back and it's time to re-gain back my life and get some real focus going. Oh yeahhhhhhh!

And Matt messaged. His son was kicking off at his ex wife's house, so he stayed there to calm him down for the sake of the younger two and to help her out. Said he missed me and would have texted me, but his daughter always uses his phone and she knows his password. Mental note - never send any remotely sexy pics to Matt if we every get to that stage. Ooh Pen, you know better than that. It's not *if*, it's *when*!

When we get to that stage. Positive thinking girl!

Not that I meant getting to the stage of sending sexy pics. No way. Not going down that troublesome pathway.

Diary, do I believe Matt? I'm not sure. I still have that same niggling feeling, but I am keeping an open mind. Gosh why is it all so complicated?

Monday 4ᵗʰ January

Bugger, shit and fanny flaps!!! Aarghhhhhh! Ben was back at school one day and then they locked the schools down again. Gutted!!!

Even Lily was upset. We finally got her actually excited to go back and BAM...they close the doors! Flipping lockdown. That's it. Not saying anymore on the subject. I know it's a mess; I know they think they are keeping a virus at bay, but what about the sanity of us parents and the sanity of our poor kids? I'm gutted - for them, for me, as I now can't work again and for the dog whose daily routines are up the creek once again. In response, I bought wine. I've already had half a bottle and it's only eight thirty. Shite. So much for bloody Dry January! I only lasted 3 days and it's a Monday night! This is going to be one heck of a soggy wet, dripping with empty bottles to keep me sane, month! Boooooooooo flipping hoooooooo ☹

I know Diary, that there are two sides of the coin always. That there are people who feel the opposite to me right now and are glad the schools are closed due to keeping the infection at bay, but I have a feeling this is going to be the hardest lockdown for most people, not least of all, children and their parents. I hope I am wrong and this won't hurt as much as it feels like it could. I am praying for more patience than I have naturally stored within me. For me and for my kids!

Right Diary, that's it! I'm doing it. I'm a flipping queen and I am declaring my feminine (or is it masculine, can't remember?) power. I AM A QUEEN!!! Whoop whoop! I refuse to let this third lockdown break me. I have got this.

<u>1.25am</u>
I shouldn't have hit the wine. It never solves anything even if it feels like a great idea at the time. Got to go to bed and sleep. Queen P is up at ridiculous o'clock tomorrow morning to take the dog out. Then do schooling. Oh why didn't I stick to Dry January? Why am I such a bad girl? Why do I let life get on top of me? Okay, too tired to remember what I asked the why about in the first place.

Tuesday 5th January

Crazy hangover on the first day of homeschooling. Oh Pen, you really should know better!

<u>1.30 p.m.</u>

Escaped upstairs whilst they eat lunch. I can do this Diary, I really can. It's all about mindset. I've been listening to Dr Wayne Dyer on my dog walk this morning. I so can do this. Do I really believe it or am I just convincing myself to feel better?

Matt messaged earlier. Asking me if I am ok because I haven't yet messaged him. As much as I am desperate to see him, I refuse to message back today. I promised myself I would not jump when he says jump, despite my desire to do so. I am strong and I can do this. I am Queen P and I will not flipping jump. I will not jump. I WILL NOT flipping jump!

<u>11.30 p.m.</u>

Had a glass of wine and messaged Matt back and now I am back to waiting for him to message me again. Argh. Why did I message? I feel I just fell off the throne I had only just ascended to. Pen you need to be stronger and have better boundaries and more self-respect!

If I could only take my own advice, I would consider training as a life coach. Until then, I am definitely the student and not the teacher.

Oh D, I sometimes feel such a mess. I'm telling this to my diary? Okay, mental note that I really am Shirley reincarnated. Oh Lordy, what and who have I become?

Wednesday 6ᵗʰ January

Got to take the dog out before 'school'. Still can't find my jeans and no chance of going to the shops to get any more. Lily gave me a pair of hers. They're a bit tight on the waist, but it's a good way to encourage me to lose weight. But where the heck did those jeans go?

5 p.m.

We renamed our wellies, *Gavs*. Funny story...

I told the kids on Monday that the wonderful Gavin Williamson the Schools Minister guy, had bent to pressure and closed all schools. I am guessing I was a little angry explaining and the word 'Williamson' must have stuck in Ben's mind.

This afternoon when asking Ben to get his wellingtons on to walk the dog, since it was pretty muddy out, he said 'Williamsons? What are they?' It took me a moment to realise the mistake and I laughed.

'Let's just call them Gavs from now on shall we?' I said with a chuckle.

I so enjoyed squelching my Gavs in the muddy puddles earlier. I might have even deliberately stepped in some dog poo just to rub it in (so to speak). Awful way to find out there's a hole in your Gavs though. Maybe Big Brother really is watching. Damn it!

Thursday 7th January

The days seem to be rolling one into the other. Aimlessly rolling and rolling. I am starting to dread getting out of bed. It's like Groundhog Day every flipping day. My routines are the same with little, if any variance. So not enjoying homeschooling, but we are getting on with it.

I am sure a psychologist could have a field day on my current life and my personal perspective on it, but right now, I know that I am only just surviving this third lockdown. I feel like I am breathing through a paper straw in a really muddy lake. One false move and I am in sinking mud sand, ready to be swallowed up by invisible teeth. Meanwhile, everyone I love is on the bank watching and willing me to keep breathing.

In the tune of Dory from Finding Nemo, I keep chanting to myself on days when Groundhog Day feels like breathing through that frail, paper straw...

Keep on breathing, keep on breathing.

Talking of swimming and fish, I think I have been neglecting the tropical fish in the tank. Okay, I confess, I KNOW I have been neglecting them. Not on purpose of course, but because they are always the last thing on my mind. The orange one looked like he was dying three days ago. But every time Lily and I try to take him out to bury him down the loo, he suddenly resurrects! This went on for three days, until this evening, the kids' dad came in and took one look at the fish tank and declared it a marine disaster. He cleaned it, changed the water and the filter and actually plugged in the plug that heated up the tank (ex reminded me that they are

179

tropical fish after all, but in my defence, I did say that I thought I pulled the plug out that charged Lily's speaker. Seems I didn't...).

I feel if there was an Oscar for a fish, then the orange one in my tank would have definitely been nominated. The poor guy had to feign death for three days to get someone to clean the bloody fish tank! Seriously Diary, it's not my fault. I can't do everything!

Wednesday 20th January

Strange day. Someone collected my old tumble dryer. Friend of a friend's dryer packed up and they have five kids: such a sweet couple and so happy to help them out in some, small way.

She sent me a message later though. Seems she found some clothes in the dryer! So that's where my missing jeans and Ben's joggers and some other bits have been hiding the past couple of months – in the old dryer in my own conservatory! I must have dried the clothes and being a combination of distracted and harassed by life, forgot to empty the dryer before unplugging it from the wall and plugging in the new one.

She dropped off the clothes in a bag when I was out walking the dog. Imagine my horror Diary, when I came back home to discover that along with all the lost clothes, were my worse pair of period pants - scaggy, holey, blood stained and a washed out shade of blue, and never destined to be seen by another person, EVER! Can my life get any more weird or embarrassing?

<u>9.30 p.m.</u>

Yes, it seems it can.

I thought I threw the pants into the bin, but they must have caught on the lid. So there they have hung all day, with the blood stained gusset outward facing. The bin sits near the front door, so that's the postman and the delivery driver, my next door neighbour who dropped off a wrongly delivered letter and my already can't look at me 76 year old neighbour, who have all probably seen them. Argh!

It was definitely a large glass of wine, bar of chocolate and half a bag of Doritos kind of night!

Friday 8ᵗʰ January

Matt messaged back with another excuse to do with his ex wife and kid. Something snapped inside me and the words 'Own your crown Queen!' rushed into my conscious brain.

I knew what I had to do. I picked up the phone. I wasn't going to respond to his ghosting by airing him back. I'm not fifteen! Instead I sent him this message:

'Matt, let's face it; you're playing me. I really don't think you and your wife are over. I think you are still in love with her and so I can't really see us ever happening. Shame as I really liked you and think we could have got on really well. Buy hey, if this past year has shown me anything, it's that shit happens and you just have to get over it! So go deliver your package to someplace

else or keep it at home. This door is permanently shut. Have a good life. Penny.'

I felt so strong, so empowered sending that message, but alas, almost the moment I sent the text, I got one back from him. I doubt he even had time to open mine before he sent his. We must have sent them at exactly the same time.

'Hi Penny. Sorry I have been so elusive. My ex wife's mum who was like a surrogate mother to me, has been very poorly. Not Covid thankfully. My wife was distraught and went to spend time looking after her. I had to take time to spend with the kids. I know I have been mucking you about and I'm really sorry. You deserve so much better than this. I need to be around for the family right now. Maybe when this is all over and we can get back out into the real world again, we can grab that drink? You've been great. Really kind and patient. I appreciate that. You're such an amazing, funny woman. Hope to be seeing you on your doorstep soon. Take care, love Matt xx.'

No words….

Diary. I am such a…

Tuesday 2nd February

Some days seem to come rolled in shit paper and today is one of those. I slept badly. Awake three times in the night and was only just getting into a deep sleep when the puppy starts barking downstairs.

These are the days when I really could do with a partner to say 'Stay in bed darling, I'll get up and sort the dog out. Go back to sleep. I'll do the homeschooling with Ben. You have a lovely rest and not think about anything. And when you wake up, I'll have a nice cuppa ready for you and make a yummy brunch? How does that sound.'

How does that sound? How does that frickin' sound right now, today, the day that came wrapped up in shit paper? Yeah it feels effing great. Bring it on!!!

Oh wait...there isn't said partner. I made him up. My hypothetical supporting 'other adult' doesn't exist. And this lockdown isn't giving anyone else the chance to get in either.

The only person getting up to let the dog out to defecate and do his peeing, is me. I'm the one logging onto the class register when I turn on the computer, because the puppy craving attention, means one of us we will usually forget. Then we have the teacher politely remind us that not signing in is the equivalent of being absent. We are here! We are just being harassed by a five months old Labrador who hasn't seen us for like 9 hours, which in dog years, if you multiply it by seven, must feel like a week to him! Erm..., is that right? What's the answer? Can't work it out. Tried momentarily, timesing everything by seven and dividing by 365 days, and then thinking about minutes in a day, then the number seven comes back into the mix. Argh!!!

Maths isn't my strong point. I think we have established that by now...

No doubt about it, today was a real crap, failing mummy day. I growled, snarled, cried, swore, cried again, snarled many more times and banged doors like a stropping teenager! I was HORRIBLE!!!

My breaking point today came when Lily let the dog in from the garden without first checking his feet. It's a given with the rainy weather we are having. He digs up the garden and invariably has mucky feet: he's a puppy after all. Unfortunately, the entrance in from outside is a freezing cold conservatory, double patio doors and then the carpeted dining/living room. Mental note – must manifest a bigger house with more affirmative language. *I live in a mansion and there are many rooms in my mansion house!* Nope, not feeling it. My house is flipping tiny!

So, Jimbo isn't checked for dirty feet. We have a towel by the door to wipe his feet. Poor dog hates it, but has learned to hand us his front paws and lie on his back to do his back ones. It's impressive how fast Labs learn. Wonder if I can teach him to wear shoes outside and leave them at the door when he comes into the house? Mmm, now there's a thought...

So he has mucky, non-towel dried paws. He gets let in and runs excited, ALL around the downstairs, getting mud all over the light beige carpet, before jumping all over the un-blanketed cream sofa. I freak. I literally completely lose it. Everyone freezes and looks terrified. I use the same expletive three times in a row, getting louder and louder each time. It's a word I rarely use at home, so I have the kids' attention! I yell at the kids to get out of my sight and add, ' Or I might end up killing someone today'. They have only ever once seen me like this and scarper as quickly as their wee feet could take them, up the stairs and into their bedrooms, slamming shut their doors in case I run up after them with a rolling pin and flatten them like playdoh!

The dog meanwhile has NEVER seen me like this and takes one look at my screwed up angry face and dashes under the chair he no longer can fit under. He doesn't let that stop him however, as the chair lifts up and literally sits on his back whilst he cowers under it.

Kids gone, I say the same expletive three more times in a row and kicked the dishwasher. For no reason other than it just was there at the time. Then I crumpled to the floor in a heap and sobbed.
That's all it took. Mucky dog paws to break this mama.

What happened? Why did I fracture and fall apart like that? I know why: I simply needed a break, before I broke, or a lie-in, or a break with some lie-ins. I need to get off the Groundhog Day overeating hamster wheel and have some respite from this sod awful and ridiculous routine.

If someone like me, who is usually so positive and uplifting can struggle, then how the hell are other parents more prone to mental health issues like depression or anxiety, dealing with it? And what of those parents with more challenging or demanding children, or parents of kids with ADHD, Asperger's or autism? How are they coping? Blimey really, how the hell *are* they coping?

Must pull myself together and remember how blessed I am. This is a blip. Recognise it for what it is – exhaustion and exasperation. Then take steps to counterbalance it. Long baths, walks in the wood, phone chats to friends, favourite chocolate, wine... hang on. That's exactly what I am doing now! The wine and the chocolate are the reason my belly hangs over my once loose jeans.

The woods I walk every morning with the dog, sunshine, rain, snow or freezing winter icicles. My midnight baths are notorious.

Must get a life! Oh wait, this is my life. Must get used to this one then. Argh!

Wednesday 3rd February

Today was another hellish day. I could throw in quite a few expletives to really explain how today went, but Diary, for the sake of my eyes reading this back in my latter grey days, I will leave it at that! I think *hellish* really kinda sums it up. And my period came, which I guess explains how I've been feeling the past few days. I thought that by my age they dried up? Oh no, not mine. I don't look my age by around ten years and my body has convinced my uterus that I am not my age either. It's still acting like I am in my late thirties!

Mind you, I needn't worry about getting pregnant. Can't have babies if you don't have nookie! Always a bonus…

It started well. I did the lockdown routine of quick meditation, prayer and waking up with gratitude in my heart. I swear it normally works. I said hello to the puppy, let him out, made my morning health drinks, did a couple of I AM affirmations and generally felt good.

Ben and I had breakfast and set ourselves up for 'school.' But then came multiplication of fractions. Arrghhhh!!! I HATE flipping fractions! Grrrrr. I mean, in my forty-seven years on earth, I have never had to know what 1 and 3/4 x 3 equals. Ben said he used to be good at maths and now it's his worse subject. I feel awful! It's because I just can't do maths. His English has improved no end though and it was his worse subject before this lockdown! That's what comes of having a published author mum at home with him. Shame for him that my book isn't in maths!

Nobody in my family except my ex can do fractions. We got the basics of it, just about, but then they threw in subtraction, division, multiplication, mixed numbers and imperfect fractions. It's like being stuck in a fraction supermarket not knowing what to buy and having no resources to buy it with!

Poor Ben. Today we sat and listened to the teacher conducting the live lesson. He and I had a sheet of paper and a pen each, as per the norm. I can tell when we are both struggling. I bite my lip, get a sweaty back and stare intently at the screen as if a computer genie were going to pop out and give me the missing answers! Ben fiddled with his pen, played with a Transformer toy, pretended to fall off his chair (three times!) and then chased the puppy round the room. The tension built. My stress levels expanded and then started climbing the walls.

'Sit down Ben and focus!' I cried out in exasperation.

He returned and sat looking sheepish, but within a couple of minutes began to lose focus and fidget with stuff again.

Meanwhile, the teacher is frustrated at the students in class not getting it. This stuff is hard and they missed out a lot of the foundations of fractions with the first lockdown last year. So Ben doesn't want to admit to the online teaching assistant that he is stuck/lost/given up the ghost. I nag him to message her as we get more and more behind the basic principles of the equations. *What don't you get Ben?* Came her reply after his 'I don't get it' message on screen. Ben and I look at each other in exasperation 'Everything!' we mutually cry out to no one listening (we are on mute).

After feeling lost in the live lesson and attempting the equations ourselves for the next one and a half hours, I felt sick with anxiety. Even my groin was sweating! Neither of us was getting it; the penny was absolutely refusing to drop into either of our brains. Ben was now running around the living room and chasing a dog that didn't want to be chased, since he was desperate for his morning walk. The dog barks, Ben barks back and I close the laptop out of sheer exasperation and declare to all of us (including the dog), 'We are taking a break. Get your Gavs on, the Woods are going to the woods!'

'Yay!' shouts Ben. 'Woof' barks the dog.

Ben and Jimbo find a little stream with an outlet. Ben had the good sense to wear his boots. Meanwhile, my Gavs have a hole in. Of course they do; they are Gavs after all!

Surrounding the stream, are old bricks imbedded into the ground in all sorts of positions. They look like they had been dumped years ago and life grew up around them. But with Ben around, their time for sleeping had ended, but then nobody ever said 'let sleeping bricks lie!' He digs them up, joined by a barking Jimbo who simply wants to hold the bricks in his mouth. This goes on for a while and I'm trying not to get stressed because we still have three lessons left to do and its already way past lunchtime. Despite the joy the two are having playing in the stream and with the bricks, my anxiety is building once again. I feel like I am living in perpetual stress right now.

This can't be healthy for the kids or the dog, to have a grumpy, snappy mummy stomping around the house? Whenever I lose my temper and start shouting or banging cupboards like a stroppy kid, the dog takes to running under my favourite antique Queen Anne blue chair. Trouble is, the Labrador is now five months old and much bigger than he was when he first started to hide under there (usually when he stole a sock or pants off the radiator!). He's grown so much that the chair now shifts up when he goes underneath. If he's not careful, he'll be wearing the chair on his back like a hermit crab!

When we get home from the outing 45 minutes later, exhausted and wet, I made the decision to not continue with the schoolwork. It was gone two o'clock and I had to get to the shops. Actually, what I really wanted, was to burst into tears, but I didn't want to cause even more stress to the children by seeing their mum in a sobbing heap on the floor once again. I called Rosa who lived local and was isolating. She urged me to pop round.

As soon as she opened her front door, I burst into tears. She ushered me in and took me back to the beginning. I was carrying a LOT of baggage it seemed. I sobbed, sniffled, dribbled and snotted my way through all the layers of things causing me either frustration or unhappiness. The dog, the kids, homeschooling (especially damn maths), loss of income, lack of income, lack of love, lack of support, lack of money, lack, lack and some more lack with cherries on the top! Damn was I feeling the lack.

Rosa put me right. She always did and usually by asking me just the one question. 'Where's the lesson?'

Damn that woman always gets me where it hurts. The lesson...

'That I can't cope? That I'm a failure as a parent?' I wailed.

'No girl. That's not the lesson, that's you projecting past shit into your present because you haven't dealt with it.'

I looked up. I knew she was right about the past stuff. I had been feeling like a failure on and off for a few years. Probably right back to the end of the marriage. I cried again. I was even worse a mess than I realised.

'So I'm dragging my past into things?' I asked.

'Yes you are. You aren't letting go of that which no longer serves you.' I must have looked be-fuddled, since she went on to explain further.

'You see, you can't really move forward until you let go of the ropes tying you to past shit. Whether that's relationships, childhood, finance, whatever it is, these things are holding you prisoner in your past. It's almost impossible to move forward if you are constantly being pulled back into the past. Do you understand?' I nodded slowly. Wiping my wet nose on the back of my sleeve like a child.

'Look at it this way. You get onto a boat. You intend to sail across to a beautiful island. The weather is perfect, you have your bag packed and you are completely ready to sail. You know where you want to go. Trouble is, your boat is tied to the moorings. You can't leave until you deliberately untie the rope.' She looks at me intently, waiting for the penny to drop.

'So I have to untie the rope before I can sail off? The rope is my past and all the things holding me back, is that it?'

She nodded. Then got up and made us tea, whilst she let that little nugget sink into my brain. I was left pondering what the rope in my life represented. I had many. My childhood, the loss of my parents, the end of my marriage, the loss of earnings (twice) and having my heart bruised by the Publishing Director. That last one accounted for why I was still single. Fear of getting hurt again was a biggie for me.

'Have you decided then if you want to hold on, or let go and sail away free?' Rosa asked as she walked in with a cute tray holding two mugs and some Jammy Dodger biscuits. Now that takes me back Diary.

We talked some more and I finished my tea and biscuits. I had food for thought for the next few days that's for sure. That Matt thing – I knew from my screaming instincts, that he was just another shield for my heart. He was never going to commit and I knew deep down that was the case and that my sub conscious was trying to protect me again by sending me someone like that who fitted into the pattern of the guy I told myself I wanted because, I didn't think I deserved someone better.

Oh boy! All this personal development stuff is so exhausting Diary. And when will I be emotionally sorted enough to be ready to meet Mr Right, if I keep choosing Mr wrong because I am too scared that I might be too wrong for Mr Right and he leaves me before I find out if we are compatible enough to work and be right for each other?

Okay I am officially lockdown crazy, because what I just wrote makes perfect sense to me even though it is completely mind-boggling!

I think I need to do more affirmations:

I AM READY TO MEET MR RIGHT
I AM READY TO LET GO OF THE ROPE
I AM GOING TO SAIL AWAY INTO THE SUNSET WITH MR RIGHT

Thursday 4th February

Lily turns 16.

Lockdown birthday number two. Poor Lily. Turning sixteen is a big deal and she got to celebrate the way she does everyday since being confined to the house – in the bloody house!

I couldn't get a balloon and wasn't going to pay £17.99 to get one delivered just because the local shops are closed, especially as I knew it would create so much noise and stress with the dog wanting to kill it. I ordered her favourite gluten free cupcakes from a local business and we got in Domino's Pizzas, despite them no longer making gluten free pizzas (why????). Good job the nachos and chicken wings are gluten free! Her sister came from London and their dad visited.

Isn't it amazing how we have learned to make do? How the majority of independent shops are closed for our safety, yet we can order anything we want online and get a delivery driver who handles packages from all over the world daily, to drop it on our doorstep? We rip open the packaging, handle it and the contents and don't think for one moment about anyone else before us, who may also have handled it? And if you have teenagers, the parcels seem to just keep coming and coming. Yet send them to school, or open up the shops...?

It's too exhausting to figure out. And expressing a questioning opinion, often results in someone jumping down your throat, for indeed expressing an opinion outside of the given narrative. So our bubbles become even more 'bubblefied' as we only entertain our own thoughts and opinions. What a crazy life we are suddenly living! Throw in a philosophical, overthinking, always questioning soul like myself and it's a recipe for a cauldron pot!

Ok Diary, I went off on one there. Reeling myself back in...

Lily's birthday... lots of lovely presents, parcels in the post (no other comment), flowers, chocs, cakes, pizza and many social media messages. We tried to make it special - a birthday banner, Moonpig cards, special tablecloth and party poppers (took an hour to clean up the next morning and I swear that's what gave the dog a cough and the resulting £65 vet bill!).

I really hope future birthdays make up for this one. Turning sixteen is a big deal for teenage girls and despite our efforts, we couldn't make up for not having her friends around her or having a party. I really pray that this is a time in kids' memories that will be painted over with better days ahead.

And with all these parcels arriving, I did notice that we have a different DPD driver. He's safe; not my type!

Friday 5th February

Wondering if I am on 'the turn'? Still crying all the time. Day three of period so I can't even blame that any longer. What if I'm hitting the menopause? Great. Throw crazy, menopausal, psychotic mum into the lockdown pie why don't you?

At least I still have periods. That means that I don't have to yet worry about menopausal 'dryness' or hot sweats, or weight gain as so many of my friends are experiencing. I just pray I meet a guy before my downstairs dries up like a grape in the sun. Oh the pity!

I would so love to meet someone right now to give some excitement back into my life. Loved having the excuse of Matt's messaging to look at my phone and giving me something to look forward to. I would rather wake up every morning feeling like I am stuck in the film 50 First Dates than stuck in this perpetually frustrating Groundhog Day every flipping day of the week! Mind you, I do think Bill Murray fell in love in the end in that film. There's got to be a rainbow at the end of this howling storm right?

Why couldn't I meet a guy like Matt, but who wasn't Matt? Someone who came with the promises of roses, romance and happy ever afters, and flipping delivered on those said promises? I'm not the only woman to want this either and from what I've seen from my men friends posting on social media, many feel the same about women. But here I am - single life and single mum. Praying neither is a forever status.

<u>11.30 p.m.</u>
It's Friday. I had cocktails. Two large ones: Bliss. So sue me.

Diary, I am certifiably lockdown doolally!

Saturday 6th February

Ben woke me up by shouting that he was cold.

'Well close the window!" I shouted back frustrated.

'Can I come in your bed?' he cried out.

'No! Go back to sleep!'

'Ok." Came the reply'

I checked my phone – 5.23am. It's pretty impossible to get back to sleep at that time. But I eventually did and went into the weirdest dream.

I was a famous author and Brad Pitt wanted to date me (you can tell it's a dream when he rocks up!). I remember the dress I wore and these weird electric blue high-heeled knee length boots that really did not go with the outfit. But in my dream I thought I looked hot. Hah!

I rocked up to my old village in Wales that I've not visited for over ten years. Why do dreams do that? Throw you back to childhood places and people that you think you've left behind? Yet it wasn't my childhood village at the same time. In fact, it was a kids' outreach camp place, situated in what looked more like an inner city London suburb, than a tiny village on the outskirts of a forest in the deepest part of a Welsh mountain valley. In the dream, I was somehow enrolled into helping teach the kids because I mentioned I was a writer. Then next thing I know, I was meeting Richard my ex, in a big house someplace else and even more bizarrely, everyone in the club, including the leaders were also there.

Considering we left on bad terms and I really try not to think about him *ever*, it was pretty weird when he got up off a huge cream sofa and beckoned me into the kitchen and once there, he asked if we could 'do it'. Blimey.

I woke up so confused. What was that all about? It was 7.12am. Everyone was sleeping, even the dog. I tried to go back in and straighten out the dream and tell my ex I was so never going to go there with him, whilst also wanting to change the boots I was wearing. I really hated those boots! You can do that in half-sleep dreams – change the whole thing round and create whatever you want. Unless you fall asleep in the process and then it all gets weird and convoluted again.

I did fall back asleep and re-entered the dream, Brad had walked in on me taking off my boots in the kitchen of this big house, just at the point when my naked ex stood in front of him with his sausage out, ready and willing for action! Thank goodness the dog woke me up at 8.18 a.m.

Talk about starting the day confused! I dragged myself up off the bed, scratching my head and wondering if I really am going insane with lockdown, or if there's a secret message hidden in the dream?

Ben came down twenty minutes later. Lily slept. I made pancakes for us, then walked the dog in the woods. I felt so perplexed by the dream, that I called David, as I was sure he would be able to help me decipher the hidden message that I was still too blind to see.

'You need to let go of the past. Your childhood, your ex, this Matt guy who was just another useless waste of space that you put in front of you to avoid waiting. Take your time and the right person for you will come along. But he won't if you keep holding onto pain and putting up barriers to protect yourself from getting hurt. It's like a repeating pattern of relationships that you keep walking into. Let them go and trust in the Universe. It really does have your back you know.'

'But why do I keep dreaming of Brad? Truthfully, I don't even fancy him!'

'It's a fantasy. You're dreaming of something you can't have because it's easier than facing reality. Let go of all that stuff that doesn't serve you and you'll be surprised by what does show up.'

Wow. I love David for getting me back on the train. Trust and patience – they sound so easy, but are so damn difficult to achieve when you have trust and patience issues!

What if it's Brad that's going to show up? Blimey! 'Wood-Pitt' Penny, just remember that!

10.50 p.m.
So much work to do on myself, but I am determined. After all, I have survived two-and-a-half lockdowns, temporary loss of everything I had built up, a marriage break up and a whole load of other crap. I can do this.

I CAN DO THIS!!!

Okay, I just screamed that out very loud, woke Ben up and sent Lily running into my bedroom to check up on me. Must remember Diary - I am a lockdown mum living on the edge and therefore likely to be prone to irrational, loud and totally out-of-character behaviour on a very regular basis! I'm normal.

Time to get rest my brain and catch some zeds!

Monday 8th February

<u>7.35 a.m.</u>

I don't want to wake up. Pleeeeease can someone take over my life today so I can stay in bed, pretend to sleep and dream of a different life to the one I am in right now?

Nope. Not happening anytime soon it seems. I am the only one awake, despite the continuation of the damned dog barking. He's not going to relent unless I get out of bed and let him out of his crate for a wee and poo. No matter how much I choose to ignore him, I have to get up, or else I will have two groaning kids on a Monday morning. Oh damn, it's Monday. Another five days of home school. Noooo!

Diary, I don't want to school today. I really don't. Where the hell did the weekend go? What's that song by The Boomtown Rats about not liking Mondays? I don't want to shoot anyone, but I could really silence a dog right now...

Ok, I am UP!!! Jeez.

<u>11 p.m.</u>

Diary. I'm back...

What a day that was. Wish I'd stayed in bed. But at least maths has moved from fractions to decimals and Ben can actually do them without needing my help. Yippee! No more maths teaching for me this week! But Lily's laptop charger broke today, so we are now all sharing my laptop. Great. ☹ And there's me thinking I could do some writing whilst Ben does the maths class on his sister's laptop before she finally gets out of bed to pretend she is going to do her schoolwork. She's a bright kid, but damn lockdown for kicking ten tonnes of shit out of her enthusiasm to do the bloody school work.

The dog's happy though as I finally get to snuggle up to him on the sofa whilst Ben does his class. It's just like we used to do before Christmas, on the days when the kids were at school. Ah...those were the days.

10 p.m.
Bit sloshed. Unusual for this time of the week, but it has been a bit of a hellish evening.

So tonight I was at a loss of what to make the kids for dinner. Feeding them three times a day almost every day and trying to make each meal different, is nigh on impossible with gluten free and practically dairy free kids, one of whom hates food touching and the other refuses to eat meat and food in sauce and neither like fish, which is mainly what I eat. Argh! I decided on homemade chicken nuggets. It's a faff, since I have to make them gluten free from scratch and it's time consuming. But Ben plays his Xbox, Lily stays in her room and Jimbo hangs around my feet waiting for scraps to drop. Plus I finally get my laptop.

So, what if I tend to drag out dinner longer that it should be, because that's the only time I get to watch my Netflix series? I may be sipping a glass of something too, whilst (slowly) chopping and dipping and coating the chicken and ignoring the pleas of 'When's dinner ready Mum?' and 'I'm starving!' And the dog whining at my feet because all he can smell is mouth watering CHICKEN!

They'll get fed soon. It's not like they haven't been emptying the snack cupboard all day, everyday since last March!

Finally, about half hour later than I said, dinner was on the table. Jimbo was locked in the conservatory and we all tried to ignore his ridiculous barking. How dare I deprive him of his favourite food – chicken!

So we all sat down. Lily and Ben bickered as was now the norm at the table. Wine helps me ignore and not react. Lily didn't like Ben picking up the nuggets with his grubby fingers (I did nag him at least four times to wash his hands, but my life has shortened considerably over the past few months, so why reduce it further with the stress of nag number five?). Lily scraped her chair on the floor making a noise and Ben moaned. And so it went on, one bicker and complaint after the other, until Ben piped up, 'Mum, where's the ketchup?'

'Dur! In the cupboard numbskull!' Lily replied with a grimace at her brother. He gets up sighing in disgrace that he actually had to go get his own ketchup.

'It's not there.' he proclaims sitting back down and sticking his tongue out to his sister. She kicks him under the table and he yells 'Ow!' and pretends to cry. Lily then mock laughs and calls him 'a stupid cry baby'. In the meantime, the dog continues to bark since all he can see and smell is chicken and nobody is eating it!

I top up my glass. The second glass of ice-cold chardonnay delicately drizzles down the back of my throat and somehow makes a diversion pit stop in my brain to give it a gentle, soothing massage. I can feel the tension oozing away. Ah, bliss. Until I am dragged out of the brain massage parlour by the words, 'Where's the ketchup? Mum, where's the ketchup?'

And then I remembered. We run out a couple of days ago and it was on my shopping list for today, but I had left said list in the car. I thought I remembered everything on my list and I did. All except the very item I had braved the shops and the queues to buy in the first place – ketchup. Oh dear.

'I forgot to buy it. Sorry,' I offered with a less than convincing, win-him-over smile.

'Well I can't eat dinner without ketchup!' came his staunch reply.

'Don't be so stupid!' Lily pitched in, spitting out the s sounds.
'You're stupid!' Ben replied close to hysteria.

'Don't have a go at me because you are a baby and can't eat nuggets without ketchup! I don't eat ketchup and I eat the nuggets.' Lily wasn't helping.

'You don't like ketchup so what do you know?' Ben pitched back.

'Well it's tough. There's no ketchup so suck it up and stop being a big baby!'

I tried to get a word in I really did, but between the two of them close to hysteria, the dog going crazy in the conservatory and desperate to get his teeth stuck into the uneaten food on their plates and my brain in zombie mode from exhaustion and a wine massage, I was failing miserably at controlling the rising stress levels at the table.

'I'm not eating it then if there's no ketchup!' Ben exclaimed pushing his plate away suddenly. Unfortunately, his plate hit his glass of water, which then hit Lily's glass and the two crashed together and sent water spilling all over Lily's plate. This simple act of defiance by a 10 year-old, escalated slight bickering, to full blown sibling war. Lily screamed at him, Ben screamed back before leaving the table, slamming the living room door and running upstairs in tears. Lily fumes in rage at the mess on her plate, which then turns to tears and when I finally have my voice heard, it's only to say the wrong thing and she also leaves the table, slams the door and stomps up into her room, crashing her bedroom door for absolute affect.

And I sit and survey the mess. My appetite for homemade nuggets and oven chips has suddenly dissipated and I get up with a sigh. I remove Lily's plate of swimming nuggets and backstroking carrots and replace it with my perfectly dry plate of food. I cover both their plates with tin foil and ignore the barking dog, who by now, is literally somersaulting in the conservatory, with drooling excitement at the discarded plates of his favourite food.

Then I nip next door and kindly ask if we can borrow some ketchup. It's Covid time, so they *give* me their ketchup and I thank them and offer to buy a replacement bottle.

I return to the scene of the crime and place the ketchup next to my son's plate. Last thing to do before calling the kids back to the table, was to place the soggy chicken nuggets in the dog's bowl and watch as he almost breaks my legs to get to his bowl when I open the door.

When the kids were finally at the table and apologies said, I retired to the kitchen to tidy up (and pour a third, much needed glass of wine).

'Where's your dinner mum?' Lily asked.

'

Oh, I ate it when you were upstairs.' I swear I saw the dog wink at me. Tomorrow I will have to buy two bottles of ketchup. I won't be forgetting my list any time soon. Maybe I should buy more wine too since I just run out?

Diary, it's great this lockdown living eh?

Tuesday 9th February

I woke up with huge anxiety today, plus a massive hangover. I rarely drink more than two glasses of wine and especially not on a weeknight.

This crushing feeling of anxiety isn't like me. I blame the crazy dream I had. I heard that many people aren't sleeping or having awful dreams during lockdown, but other than dreams about being in lockdown or about Brad Pitt, I hadn't yet experienced anything I could call really 'weird'. That changed with last night's dream.

Satan and his minions rose up from the earth. But it wasn't the big red devil type character we are familiar with in stories, you know - the one with the anchor tail, the horns and scaly back, looking, well, 'devilish', whilst holding a pitchfork. No, this one was wearing a suit and a red tie and bumbling in a monologue style not dissimilar to a voice one might hear in an Eton type private school and certainly like one from the halls of Westminster. This devil's voice droned on about my 'despicable sins' and barking on that I would 'never be seeing the cold light of day again'.

His minions all wore suits and were as equally pernicious, with sickly pale faces, round black glasses over piercing beady eyes, balding, shiny heads and the deepest, dark purple circles that resembled moon craters, under their eyes. All grey or navy suited looking grave and shaking their head with the recrimination of a judge about to give the death penalty to a guilty criminal. But there was no criminal in the dock: just myself. I was sitting on my sofa, except it wasn't mine, but the one from my mum's house from when I was a kid (see, the childhood home stuff coming back to haunt me? What the flip is that all about? Freud would have a field day on me!). There I sat, being sentenced by these drab, looming, statuesque judges. My crime was apparently so heinous that the judgement was indefinite confinement.

However, I wasn't begging for forgiveness, or mercy, or cowering with self-pity, nor remorse. Instead, I simply looked up from where I sat and shouted 'No!!!' The devil leader, who seemed to have grown to a hundred foot, bent over and peered into my pertinacious face. His rat-like eyes pink and beady, attempted to poke into my sub-conscious and feed off my guilt, but there was no guilt forthcoming.

"What is my crime?" I asked in defiance.

"Hah! You dare to ask *me* that?" he bellowed back. The force of his words whooshed my hair back behind my face, which felt as though it were being torn apart by the bitterness of his words and the miasmic, rancid stench of his breath.

He beckoned one of his suited minions over and commanded him with unspoken words, to read out the crime for which I was to be punished.

"You didn't buy ketchup and thus ruined last night's dinner!" came the reply.

I felt all their eyes bore down at me. My conspirators had already had me judged and sentenced. I was a bad mama and going to hell for eternity: lockdown forever for me. How could I forget the bloody ketchup? It was on my list for goodness sake! On my bloody list!!!

I woke up in a sweat. Blimey.

I quickly got out of bed and wrote KETCHUP in big black letters on a notepad that sat on my trunk next to my bed, for those rare times that inspiration struck me. I wasn't going to forget to buy ketchup today that's for sure!

The day did get better, though I retained a quiet state of twisting anxiety that gnarled at my insides all day. The dream, albeit surreal and inconceivable, remained an unwanted companion by my side. Somewhat like a burp that's stuck and can't come out no matter how many times you false burp to explode the bubble. And then that false burp makes the need to burp even worse as now you are left with two burps needing to be released, or just one big massive belch if you try the false burp thing again in the hope to explode the other two!

Did I really just write that? Oh D... I need to get a life. I need to get out and work, or see people and have some bloody grown up conversation time. Lockdown is destroying my brain as well as my peace of mind at night.

That devil really did look familiar...

Wednesday 10th February

Hump Day! Oh boy do I wish I could hump today ☹

I am so missing human contact and especially close (very close) contact. Watching my dog hump what remains of his toy 'girlfriend', doesn't exactly make me want to have 'relations', but it reminds me that there is someone for everyone. Jimbo shagging the life out of a wretched life sized cuddly toy Labrador, which is missing a nose, ears, eyes, a tail, a tongue and now a quarter of its fluffy white infilling insides, is pretty gross, but come one, at least he's happy!

Oh, to have a romance going on right now. Not thinking of Matt, not thinking of Matt. Matt who? See...not at all thinking of someone called Matt I don't even know. Blimey. I am CRACKING UP!

Moving on from Matt. Who's Matt again? Argh.

I know I keep saying this Diary, but lockdown does make me feel lonely and missing having a special someone. I would so love to have someone to message. Even if we couldn't meet up, we could Facetime. It's apparently what many couples are doing if they can't actually meet. Who'd have thought that a year ago; so weird. However, it would give me a reason to do my hair and put on some make up. I swear that security guard in Sainsbury's thinks I fancy him the way I saunter in with mascara and blush. I gave up on lipstick months ago since it kept coming off onto my mask and then I'd be wearing it on my chin, but at least I still have some semblance of lashes lurking out from under my bobble hat! At least I still try for goodness sake!

I had to venture out to the bank last week. So I put on a skirt and my long leather boots and my posh coat, did my hair and put on make up. I bought myself a hot chocolate I couldn't drink inside the bank because of wearing a bleeding mask, but at least I made an effort! I didn't see anyone I know which was a shame as I felt my effort was wasted, but I did feel good and that's what mattered really. Though I did get changed into my joggers again as soon as I got home!

How am I going to adjust again to the real world when I am back out there working and socialising? I already panic about what to wear as it is and I rarely see anyone unless they are standing in a supermarket queue or walking a dog. Neither is an excuse to get dressed up.

I NEED TO GET OUT OF LOCKDOWN, NOWWWWWW!!!!!

Thursday 11th February

It was freezing today. We've all had enough of the snow and the cold spell. Storm whatsherface can go do one now thank you! The novelty of throwing snowballs and making snowmen, wore off a few weekends ago when we got our first snow flurry. Now it's just bloody freezing and slippery and there's only so much sniffing my constant pink nose can deal with when walking the dog at minus 2 degrees every morning.

I can't knock the dog walking though. It does get me out of the constant daily mum demands. Cooking, shopping, baking, making, cleaning (the minimal), washing (constant), drying, putting clothes away, making beds, stocking up the loo rolls, hours of homeschooling, hours of listening to bickering, or the bored dog barking to go either in or out of the garden, constant nagging, perpetual attempts at persuading daughter to open up her laptop to work; the tears, the laughter, the nagging for me to look at this, look at that, fetch me this, make me that... every single day except for four days a month when they are at their dad's.

And then I miss them! What is it with that? You think I would be running round the house naked laughing my head off with a large bottle of whatever singing 'No kids! No Kids! No kids!' But no, not me, the moment they leave, I feel sadness and loss. Perhaps if I actually had someplace to go, someone to see or even something to do, I wouldn't feel that way? And besides, last time I walked around the house naked, I nearly gave a 76 year-old man a heart attack!

Being a parent is the weirdest job of all. It never makes sense, conjures up all sorts of bizarre experiences and emotions, is the most difficult, confusing, anxiety driving job of all, yet is also the most beautiful, rewarding and fulfilling blessing.

But sometimes, I would like a lie in. Just saying.

And someone to make me a cup of tea once in a while. Must train the kids to look after me. Last time I had a cuppa made for me, was when I bashed my head and thought I was going to die. Extreme way to get a cuppa made for me it must be said! Still got the lump to prove it.

Friday 12th February

Dropped Lily off to her sister's for the weekend. It's the first time ever. She was struggling with her bedroom to kitchen and back again existence. She definitely needed the break for her mental wellbeing. She has all but given up on school and it's her GCSE year. I have tried everything in my motherly powers to encourage, coerce, implore and threaten my middle child to do the work, but she simply says 'maybe tomorrow' and hides back in her room. Argh.

She was doing so well at school too and on target for ten GCSEs this summer. Letting go of the control of this situation, *her* situation, has been so challenging for me, the control freak mummy. I had to fight for my education and here I am, witnessing helplessly, as my daughter seemingly discards hers. I know why she's like this; it's the anxiety of doing the work online and the hopelessness she feels about life and her future. The teenagers are more researched than most adults and the suspicion they hold for *Those That Think They Know Best*, coupled with the way they feel society points the finger of blame at them for literally being at school, means that their mental health on the whole, is like a ticking time bomb for so many. The situation literally sends her into panic attacks. Its so hard to witness and another reason for my frustration with them not being at school. She keeps informing me of kids her age who are so depressed they often discuss suicidal thoughts and so many are now anaesthetising with drugs or self harm. My heart goes out to them, it really does.

So I am not as hard on her as I could be as her mother. I have had to become kinder and more considerate. That has been so bloody hard! Did I mention I was a control freak? Sooo hard!

With Lily at Saskia's, it was just Ben and I this weekend and we had such a great day together. We visited my bubble friend – the joy of being a single parent household is that we are able to have a bubble friend. Thank you Universe for the smallest of beautiful gifts that actually means so much. I switch off my mummy mode button for a short while and sit with a cuppa *made by someone else* and a real, proper chinwag, whilst Ben got to play with her daughters. Oh the small things that can make us happy.

10.20 p.m.
He's finally asleep after us watching Wonder Woman, walking Jimbo to the shop with me to satisfy my diet coke craving and then taking it in turns to hula hoop to Eminem, Post Malone and Lil Nas X. Guess that's what happens to a kid's music tastes, when they have teenage sisters and the nineteen year old is working at being a hip hop singer songwriter!

Time for a very large glass of wine and some Netflix: definitely brain-numbing time. Night diary…

Sunday 14th February

Valentines Day. It's my weekend without the kids and only the dog to give my love to. How ironic that every Valentines Day, birthday and Christmas since being single, I have spent without being with a guy. Today is no different.

Imagine my shock then, when a beautiful bunch of deep red tulips and a bottle of Veuve Cliquot champagne, was nicely wrapped and left anonymously on my doorstep! I don't know if I was more overjoyed at being left such an amazing gift, or frustrated that my secret admirer didn't leave a calling card.

Who could it be? I went through all the possibilities and was left with two guys. Matt was discounted since he hadn't even replied to my last text (no surprise there). I also discounted Richard since that wasn't his style.

Only two other possible guys left to choose from and both have girlfriends. Now that left me in a real quandary. Who out of my male friends would have left such an obviously romantic and well thought out gift and with no message or card? This lack of message discounted it being a friendship and supportive thing. I don't think it's my back this guy is thinking of having…

So what should I do? I had no evidence that it was either guy, yet my instincts told me it was. Have I somehow encouraged their fondness of me to see more than friendship? Or maybe it's impossible to have a friend who is the opposite sex? What a pickle. Blimey. What am I supposed to do knowing that?

I opened the bottle of course! Happy bloody Valentine's Day to me. And whichever guy it was, I flipping hope you treated your girl as well as you treated me today. You have the weirdest perspective on love and loyalty, but they are beautiful flowers and gorgeous fizz. Cheers and thank you for making me both cringe and smile at the same time.

And as a side note, if I find out at a later stage that these gifts are from a single male admirer, I apologise to the non-single guy friends I am thinking it might be. And thank you to the single male friend or admirer that I hadn't thought of before just now. Man, why couldn't they have just left a note and then I wouldn't be in such an over thinking tizzy? Life is so complicated.

9.50 p.m.
Oh boy. I think I will finish the bottle tomorrow, but for now I am going to regress into a numbed zombie state and wake up tomorrow actually speaking and thinking some sense.

What if I have a new disease caused by being in lockdown? What if this new disease is actually much worse than the virus itself? Bloody hell. Now that's a scary thought. What if this disease makes you overthink, write a load of old tosh to a diary and then your brain explodes at the end? Blimey O' Riley, I'm flipping doomed!

I have definitely been too long in lockdown, Diary. I am actually starting to scare myself!

Monday 15th February

Half term week! And the first three days are forecast rain. You've got to love living in Britain sometimes. It isn't so much fun right now it has to be said. I think I would rather be the family that emigrated to New Zealand a year ago, but that's hindsight for you!

I saw a few mums on social media complain about it raining over half term. That shows me three things –

1. We all hate homeschooling so much we are desperate for an excuse to leave the house
2. We are just desperate to leave the house
3. We have an opportunity to finally leave the house and we complain about the bleeding British weather

Let's face it, it always seems to rain at half term, bank holidays and the entire month of August, which is when you've finally managed to book a week's camping in Cornwall after all your non-kid friends with amazing tans, have been having the best June and July of their lives because a) they weren't penalised for taking their kids out of school during term time b) they are a family that could actually afford a foreign holiday with the kids at peak travel times. I've enjoyed the latter with my kids twice, but then I am good at finding bargains even in peak holiday times!

Half term rainy weather - oh the irony of life bites at my swollen lockdown ankles every time.

Which reminds me. Who needs shackles to keep you tied to the house when you have developed cankles that restrict movement above one mile per hour anyway? Lockdown weight gain is such a great put off for wanting to laze around in a bikini on a beach in Port somewhere or other and where the idea of 'slipping' into a wetsuit to ride some waves, when your suit no longer fits like it did last summer, is like something from a Cardi B song – you got in and you're never coming out again. I don't think she was talking about wearing a wetsuit though and I am NEVER watching that video again. Can't believe Saskia made me watch it, just so she could video my face! Okay I admit I may be a prude, but damn it, that was on another level for me!

That's what happens to middle aged mums of teenage girls into their music – we listen to all the words. I think I have a permanent neck strain from all the cringing I do in the car when I hear the lyrics from these artists. Hip hop and grime takes my neck strain winces and eye brow raising to whole new proportions. Give me Wham and Duran Duran any day of the week. Yes, I concede that I am old and I am so owning that old girl tee-shirt!

Maybe I should start blasting sounds of the 80's and 90's at home and get them into my music rather than have theirs imposed on me? If I am going to hear the F word in my house on a regular basis, I'd rather it came from me shouting at the dog when he runs onto my cream sofa after he's been digging up the garden, than I would having it blasted into my ears everyday!

Okay, now I am singing 'Relax don't do it, when you want to go to it' round the house. Ah those were the good old days: records getting banned for subtle suggestion. What would an artiste have to do these days to get their record banned from public viewing? Mmm..., call me ancient, but not sure some of the changes over the decades have been that positive.

'What was that song you were singing Mum?" Ben asked walking in on me wiggling my ass in the kitchen.

'Oh a song from my childhood. Don't think you've ever heard it?'

'Nah. Well not the way you sing it anyway. Hah!'

10.45pm

Actually getting to bed early tonight. Everyone went to bed by nine thirty, which is amazing. We are all chilled and ready for lazy mornings and lazy afternoons and even lazier evenings. With lots of dog walking and a few trips to the skate park thrown in. Now we have Prime videos, it will keep us entertained more as a family in the evenings, especially now I am not writing. Taken a break for the week to enjoy just being me. I know they will be back to school soon and despite knowing it's saving both my sanity and theirs, I also know that I will miss their company in the daytime.

Diary, I have hardly drunk any alcohol the past few days. I don't feel the need for it. Not that I need it anyway, but it has definitely become a bad habit that I slipped into. Okay, not so much slipped, as dived head first with no armbands or anchor!

When the kids go back, I am detoxing my liver, starving my belly and definitely dying my roots!

Friday 19th February

My overthinking is going way off scale at the moment. Lockdown has seen my inner critic tackling my nice inner meditation guru more times than a scrum half in a Wales international rugby match! Ooh I love a good Welsh game. All that sporting testosterone and red jerseys. Pure sport watching bliss!

Yesterday I got a message from a male contact on social media. He's very attractive and someone I met in my working life about fifteen months ago. He wanted a mutual friend's contact details. We chatted a while. Seems he and his girlfriend split up last summer. He readily supplied this information without prompting. It was such a friendly chat and we left it open for meeting up for a coffee 'when this is all over'. Boy do I dread hearing those words since who knows when it will be over?

And then my mind goes into overdrive. Was he contacting me as an excuse to connect with me again? Did he fancy me? How do I follow this up and should I leave it to him to make the next move? Where would we meet and how and if and when will lockdown ever be over and if so, will we be able to not wear a mask, or touch, or even bloody look at each other? Surely it's a matter of time before they say it can be transferred via eyeballing another person?

So much overthinking on just one tiny thing that happens to occur out of the ordinary, Groundhog Day to-day living! Will I ever be the same again, or stay this angsty, living on my nerves, slightly paranoid, one hand in the snack cupboard new version of me I feel I have become?

Maybe they'll create a new TV programme called I'm in Lockdown, Get Me Out of Here!

I'm not going on that's for sure, even if they beg me.
Okay Pen, relax, you will never be asked.

I'm a mad, overthinking single mum in lockdown...PLEASE get me outta here!!!!

Monday 22nd February

Soooo Diary...

Today we got a road map to freedom. Isn't it amazing that we are today, meant to be excited and grateful, to see our natural human rights being handed back to us one crumb at a time? If someone had mentioned a year ago that we would be jumping up and down for joy, to be told that in just four months from this date, there would be no penalties for hugging granny, or having a pint in the pub with a friend AND that we would be eternally grateful for the privilege, I think most of us would have laughed in their faces and called them a quack.

But...here we are!

Let's get the jumping for joy out of the way right now... the kids are going back to school in two weeks. Yesssss!!! It might not make everyone happy, including many of the kids, but I for one, am ecstatic, relieved and cancelling my wine monthly subscription! My liver is profusely thanking our inglorious leaders also!

Not sure what to think about it to be honest though, this road map of freedom business. I have my views, but then nobody I know has been ill with the disease and thankfully I know of no one who has sadly lost their life. I have no ageing parents and none of us are vulnerable. One thing I have learned since this pandemic officially began last March though, is that depending on our own personal circumstances, so many of us hold differing views. Some disagree or refuse to follow the narrative and yet some uphold the narrative to the crossing of t's and dotting of I's. And that's the way it is.

What has immensely concerned me, is the dissention and vehemence that one person can hold against another through intolerance of differing opinions. The hatred, anger, bitterness and accusations that I have witnessed throughout the past ten months, mainly on social media and in the media, have both shocked and saddened me to the core. Vitriol and judgement have seemingly arisen from fear and uncertainty caused by our situation. And it's understandable. There has been so much fear, which is probably the darkest force surrounding humanity in this world right now.

So how will humankind recover? How will we be able to return to any semblance of past normality knowing that this vein of fear could turn neighbour against neighbour at any given crisis?

For me, it's been keeping myself sane (though that could be debated), acknowledging that at times I have felt incredibly lonely, watching my kids struggle with their own loneliness and depression and seeing friends go into rabbit holes and struggle. Those have been the toughest parts. Yet despite this, I have striven to remain grateful. I am aware, that the thoughts, feelings and emotions caused by the past year, are going to need unpacking for quite sometime to come.

So what has been the main lesson I have gleaned from all this? That's the biggest question to myself that I am asking right now Diary. And as much as the words, hope, faith and trust rise to the forefront of my brain, the word that really comes forward, is gratitude.

Despite how much many of us have lost, including loved ones, there is much to be grateful for. We live to see another day and hopefully, have learned that bit more about who we are, both individually and collectively.

At least I can now call a poo what it really is! BJ has left the bathroom. I could tell it was him from the long, straggly blond hair he'd left hanging over the toilet! However, I am hoping that now Spring has the promise of warmer weather, my Gavs will be ensconced in the garage for another winter season to come. Perhaps, and please God no, another future season of discontent?

Finally Diary, in the words of my favourite Greek philosopher Epictetus,

'It's not what happens to you, but how you react to it that matters.'

Not sure if I can say I have responded the best I could have, but I tried. I really bloody tried.

Role on March 8th and June 21st, I'm getting ready for you!

Arise O Phoenix Mum

Broken, battered and bloody,
Elbow to hand, knee to foot,
She rose.

From ashen ground,
Scarred by battle,
She stood.

Armoured and ready for life,
An end in sight to all this strife,
She sighed.

Tomorrow in sight,
She steels her gaze,
Ready with all her might.

Packed lunches made,
Uniform pressed,
Kids back to school;
Oh, she is impressed.
Phoenix lady rises up
Once again, to fill her cup.

But she will not cry,

She will not bow down,

Or in in sadness lie.

Phoenix Mum will rise.

High above discarded bottles

And empty packets.

Far away from bickering, wanton lies;

A Universe apart from snacking cupboard hell,

So she can live to tell,

Of better days to come

And not of jailbird, lockdown mum.

Paula Love Clark

THE END

ACKNOWLEDGEMENTS

To my children Harriet, Lauren and Zac: For all those wonderful, fun, exciting, adventurous and awful moments we share. I thank you and love you beyond any words. I am incredibly blessed and grateful to have you as my children.

Thank you to David P Perlmutter, Best Selling Author and actor. Without that conversation in early January, this book would never have been born; for helping me along this book's journey and for the perpetual encouragement to achieve the end result, along with your unwavering belief that I could in fact, get the job done. For all this I am grateful.

To the gorgeous Gemma Loughlin Pepper @gemmapepperillustrations for creating the perfect illustrations for Penelope Wood and her family and for bringing alive *The Diary of a Lockdown Mum*. Sooo grateful.

To Celia for always picking up the phone and being an amazing sounding board for my ideas, my concerns and so many of my crazy thoughts. I am so grateful.

To John for continually getting me always back onto the train, even when I feel like giving up on the journey! I am grateful.

To Philip for the help with focusing my mindset, when fear was biting at my ankles: I am grateful.

To Sara, for always encouraging and supporting me and buying my books even if they are sometimes a little 'out there' and risqué. You know that I love you and am always grateful for you.

To PJ and your emotional support and belief in me. A book per brick is our motto! I am so grateful for the part you played in getting me here.

Finally, to all my friends and girlfriends who continually support me with your love, friendship, encouragement and unwavering belief. This quote is for you:

'Friendship is born at that moment when one person says to another: 'What? You too? I thought I was the only one.' ~ C.S. Lewis